Book V

Ask Jesus

Also by

Marisa Moris and Joseph Moris

Answers – Heaven Speaks

The Bible Speaks Series
Conversations with Jesus and the New Testament Authors

Book I
Matthew and Mark

Book II
Peter and John

Book III
Luke and Paul

Book IV
James and Jude

Book V
Ask Jesus

Book VI
Jesus' Parables for a 21st Century

The Bible Speaks
Conversations with Jesus and the New Testament Authors

Ask Jesus

Book V

Featuring

Jesus and a few friends

By

Joseph Moris
Marisa Moris

Book V   Ask Jesus

This book is dedicated to
Jesus Yeshua Christ
and all those "up there" who believe in this journey

The Bible Speaks

Copyright © 2015
Joseph P. Moris and Marisa P. Moris
Published by Intuition Publishing
Printed in the United States of America

ISBN-13:978-0989885171 (Intuition)
ISBN-10:0989885178

Intuition Publishing
1054 2nd Street
Encinitas, CA 92024

info@discoverintuition.com

Format and Cover by Roger C. Bull and Marisa Moris
Edited by Joseph Moris
All rights reserved.

The contents of this book may not be reproduced in any form, except for short extracts for quotation or review, without the written permission of the publisher.
© Joseph P Moris and Marisa P Moris
First Published by Intuition Publishing
Transcriptions by Monica Harris and Lorna Mulbach
Printed in the United States of America
First Edition: November 2015

20 19 18 17 16 15 14 13 12 11 (??????)
Library of Congress Cataloging-in-Publication Data
The Bible Speaks
Joseph P Moris and Marisa P Moris
p. cm. ISBN 10: 0989885178 1.) Religion 2.) Spirituality 3.) Christianity

Book V   Ask Jesus

Ephesians 4:2-5   King James Version
Author: Paul

With all lowliness and meekness, with longsuffering, forbearing one another in love; endeavoring to keep the unity of the Spirit in the bond of peace.

There is one body, and one Spirit, even as you are called in one hope of your calling:

One Lord, One Faith, One Baptism, One God and Father of all, who is above all and through all and in you all.

Ephesians 4:2-5   As paraphrased in Heaven Speaks
by: Joseph Moris

Always be humble and gentle. Because of your love, be patient with each other, making allowance for each other's faults.

Make every effort to keep yourselves united in the Spirit, binding you together with peace.

There is one body and one Spirit, just as also, you have been called to one glorious hope for the future.

Introduction

A Message from Jesus to Joe and Marisa

(Jesus) *"You may do unto this (next) book what you would like to do, but I place before you my words, I place before you my honor and I place before you my knowledge in that which I can bring to you. For I can bring it to you as Yeshua the man; I can bring it to you as Christ, that which is the Holy Christed being of God; I can bring it unto you as the spirit of man, and I can bring it to you as God. So you must first understand what you would like to be telling the world in this next book.*

For you may interview me, you may ask me questions about who I am, and what my life was about, but there are many speculations about my life already and who I was, and what I did. But bringing about the examples, bringing about, as they say, parables to explain to people who they are, why they are here, where they are going, where their loved ones are, where they are going in their life, are different ways they can learn to live a life in an honest fashion, but also live with the love of God within their heart, understanding and knowing that love is unconditional, love is light, light is ever withstanding to that which is darkness.

So know and understand that this will be a ministerial book indeed in that people will read it to feel good. People will read it to understand. People will read it to say, 'Oh, that's what they mean.

Book V   Ask Jesus

Oh, Jesus was the man, His higher self was Christ. I understand this now. Oh, this is understandable for I understand, and I understand as a man."

I, Jesus, lived this life not knowing who I was or where I was going, or where I had come from. And, I was told exactly, told exactly where I came from and where I was going, but I still did not believe, for I was a man. And just as each person is told on this planet: 'You are here for great things. You are here. You are god. You are a creator. You're a co-creator of God and you can create whatever you would like.' But does anybody know what they want to create? Gosh, no. They do not know because they do not know why they are here.

So if they were to understand the inner workings of the way that things are structured, if they were to understand the inner workings of their soul, of their soul body inside, and know how they can create a life of their dreams, this is something we would like to bring through. But know and understand that I brought ministry to a world of darkness. The two of you bring ministry to a world of darkness. And I would love to be a part of bringing this ministry, of bringing this happiness, of bringing this joy, of bringing this faith, and bringing laughter to the world; the world that does not know much laughter. We will bring the joy and the peace and the reverence to a world that feels as if it has no hope. For, we can bring examples, we can bring these parables into people's lives so that they may truly understand why they do the things they do, why they feel the things they feel.

Why does a wife get angry at her husband? Why does she get angry? Why does a man get angry? Why do they think that the world is coming to an end, when their emotions have gotten the best of them? It is because human beings, human beings are designed to have these emotions, and souls are designed to overcome these emotions. Why do you think that the sins, the sins that are listed in the Bible are many of the things caused by human emotion, caused by human greed, caused by human ego?

For, we will bring an understanding to people as to who they are, why they are here, and where they are going and it will be fun. We will bring joy into the world and people will love it. And this is something that I will enjoy doing. But as I have said, and I will continue to say, this is your book, this is your writings, and just as we have worked so many lives together, I will allow you to do what you would like to do.

I will allow you to do exactly what you would like to do for we have worked well together in many lives prior and we have collaborated together in many lives prior. For, you will remember the days, some day, when we were in Egypt. You will remember the days that we sat upon the pillars of the sun and we sat and we stared upon, we stared upon the pillars that brought unto us where the sun would set and where the sun would rise, for we were astronomers together. And this was a fun life. We were astronomers and we brought about the placements of the sun, the placements of the planets, and we gazed upon the stars each night, and you wrote about it, you wrote about it and you tried to explain it so much and then when we entered into spirit you said, 'Oh gosh, I can't believe I didn't remember that.'

So, just know, just know and understand, that each life that is lived, you will go onto being on this side where I stand at this time and say, 'I can't believe I didn't remember.' But I bring these words unto you through this channel, through your daughter in this lifetime, as the two of you have chosen, so that we can bring the ministry to this world, and this is something that I take great pride in, and I believe that you do, too, and I bless each one of you.

Book V Ask Jesus

Appreciate the brotherhood and sisterhood in which we have created over time. I bless you and bid you a good night."

The Bible Speaks: Conversations with the New Testament Authors

Table of Contents

1.	*The Holy Spirit*
2.	*Forgiveness*
3.	*The Snow Globe Introduced*
4.	*Construction of the Bible*
5.	*Parable of the Orange*
6.	*The Higher Self*
7.	*Bible 'Bloopers' vs. The Bible Speaks*
8.	*'I Am that I Am', Gabriel and the Parable of the Golf Course Part I*
9.	*The Duality of the Human Condition*
10.	*Paul and Guilt*
11.	*The Light of Christ*
12.	*The Soul's Consciousness*
13.	*Healing the Physical Body with Energy*
14.	*Securing and Discovering Truth*
15.	*The Image and Likeness of God is not Human*
16.	*What Would You Do?*
17.	*A New Consciousness*
18.	*A Son, A Brother, A Friend*
19.	*Mother Mary and the Virgin Birth*
20.	*With Personal Growth Can Come Fear*
21.	*Emmanuel*
22.	*Jesus Hears God's Voice for the First Time*
23.	*Jesus on Jude*
24.	*Parable of the Orchard*
25.	*Truth vs. Belief: An Admonition to Joe*
26.	*You Can Be Free*
27.	*Mary Magdalene and the Divine Feminine*
28.	*Parable of the Dog's Toy*
29.	*"Why God Have You Forsaken Me?"*
30.	*The Coming of Christ*
31.	*Parable of the Strawberry*
32.	*Muhammed*

33.	*Names in Biblical Times*
34.	*Jesus' First Healing*
35.	*James the Just*
36.	*Zippers*
37.	*Joseph, Mary and the Virgin Birth*
38.	*Mary and Joseph's Lost First Child*
39.	*Miracles and a Premature Birth*
40.	*Compassion*
41.	*The Human Mind is like a Satellite Dish*
42.	*Introducing Judas*
43.	*Everyone Has a Plan*
44.	*Women and Men are Equal in God's Eyes*
45.	*Mary Lived to be 102 and Joseph 87*
46.	*Spiritual Amnesia and Your Plan*
47.	*"These are the Shoes in Which I Walked"*
48.	*"Jesus be with Me"*
49.	*Curiosity*
50.	*Religion*
51.	*Parable of the Radio Station*
52.	*Parable of the Light Bulb*
53.	*The Higher Self / The Soul of Jesus*
54.	*Worshiping*
55.	*The Spirit of the Bible*
56.	*The Snow Globe*
57.	*Parable of the Hologram*
58.	*Humor*
59.	*More on Humor*
60.	*Scribes*
61.	*Parable of the Radio and the Hard Drive*
62.	*Is it Evil to Hear Your Voice?*
63.	*Forgiveness*
64.	*Parable of the Baby Monitor*
65.	*Who Created Christ?*
66.	*Must you be Christian to Have Christ?*
67.	*Multi-Dimensionality*
68.	*The Return of Jesus*
69.	*Peter and Jesus are Funny Together*

The Bible Speaks: Conversations with the New Testament Authors

70.	*I'm a Victim! Is this all there is?*
71.	*Prayer*
72.	*Advice to Pastors and Teachers*
73.	*Parable of the Mannequin*
74.	*Parable of the Human Suit*
75.	*Denying Christ*
76.	*"Break a Leg"*
77.	*The Military of God*
78.	*Mutant Humans*
79.	*Parable of the Orange and the Parallel Universes*
80.	*Parable of the 12 Story Building*
81.	*Parable of the Golf Course Part III*
82.	*The Earth Grid and the Grand Experiment*
83.	*Change in 'Spirit'....Change in Life*
84.	*Earth and God's Plan*
85.	*Jesus' Humble Message*
86.	*Never Assume How Someone Feels*
87.	*The Council of 24*
88.	*Masculine and Feminine*
89.	*Revelation: John's Parable of the Golf Course Part IV*
90.	*Halos*
91.	*Witchcraft*
92.	*Communication via the Holy Spirit*
93.	*On a Mission*
94.	*Parable of the Diamond*
95.	*Rosemary on Jesus*
96.	*Life and the Times Aren't So Different*
97.	*I am Proud of the Human Race*
98.	*The Bible is a Book of Faith*
99.	*Mark's take on Jesus*
100.	*God Would Die for Us*
101.	*Charisma*
102.	*"I came to change the World"*
103.	*Human Nature vs. Enlightenment*
104.	*We Love the Human Beings*
105.	*The Way, The Truth and The Light*
106.	*Parable of the Tennis Ball*
107.	*Jesus' Closing Comments*

1

(Snow Globe)

The Holy Spirit

(Jesus) *The Holy Spirit is the life inside of us. And Christ is the mind within us. So Christ brings the knowledge and truth and the Holy Spirit brings life.*

2

(Snow Globe)

Forgiveness

(Jesus)   When you stop looking at it as "I" am forgiving you, and look at it as "You" are forgiving you, for as your guide so eloquently put it, we are all one. For when you look at yourself as a piece of me and you're asking for forgiveness, you are truly just releasing negative energies from your, as you say, "Snow globe." You are releasing these negative energies because you say "I am done with these. They are not mine anymore. This is gone."

So the reason why people hold onto these things is because, just as we have just said, they feel unworthy. And there is no recognition, nothing is shown to them that is tangible that says "Good job for asking for forgiveness, you passed, you're approved." So, one must just truly believe that they are forgiven, and understand that when living on the earth plane, when living in physicality, mistakes are made. Mistakes are made, indeed. So when you ask how you forgive yourself for things that you have done, you do not even need to ask, so to speak, you just know that I have already forgiven you.

3

(Snow Globe)

The Snow Globe

Jesus says to do unto others as you would have them do unto you. This has been his finest lesson but he now says that the snow globe is going to change the world.

The Bible Speaks: Conversations with the New Testament Authors

4

(Luke and Paul)

Construction of the Bible

Marisa: *Jesus brings an example of how he worked with Constantine to bring about the Bible by using the snow globe.*

(Jesus) *Constantine was not a bad person. Most of his incarnations as a being, along with his soul group were other worldly, from other worlds. Planet Earth had come to a point where there was much suffering and they (*incarnating *souls from the same Constantine Soul Group) needed to bring in very intellectual-like, smart-evolved souls to come in so that they could tune into the divine mind and change the world. Constantine and members of his soul group came as humans with a plan to tune into the higher self and into the divine mind so they could bring through important spiritual information; they felt like lightning rods bringing in information. A lot of the royalty at the time, even the really bad ones, were placed on Earth as high-vibrating souls. Even though many were, as humans, bad leaders, the ones that were even merciless killers were still very integral in bringing through the information that they eventually needed to compile the Bible.*

Just having a soul that's on the Earth plane living as a human isn't enough though. There needs to be a connection and an awareness. Sometimes it takes extra effort by the soul group to bring to these earth bound souls/spirits the information, direction

and plans they need. For example: If someone is within their Snow Globe and they are not allowing information into their field, if someone is not allowing information into their Snow Globe, many times a member of the soul group will incarnate for anywhere between a day to a week to even sometimes a couple months into a woman who is also incarnated with the spirit of the same soul group, be conceived into this woman but she may lose the child. For in that case the soul brings spiritual messages into the woman's Snow Globe through the fetus. The woman now has this soul, another soul inside her body and it's like she's absorbing all the messages she needs and it's placing her on the right path to educate others.

The Earth is like this woman and so too is the Bible. The earth as well as the Bible have snow globes. We have placed a soul within the Earth in order to bring the messages we want the people of earth to learn, to know and to understand. These messages come in the form of energy for we have used the grid example and the use of soothing classical music being played within the grid.

The Bible too has a spirit. Everything has a spirit if you want to speak of a spirit as energy. So look at it as every single thing that exists on this planet has a snow globe. And every single snow globe has a different vibration and different voltage of light bulb. So the Bible carries its own snow globe and this is a much higher vibration than any man can truly tap into, that any many can truly, truly accomplish in a lifetime, or a vibration that man can accomplish.

5

(Luke and Paul)

Parable on the Orange

(Jesus)   Dear Brethren, as we convene here today and we speak of these things, you must understand that the truth lies within my heart and that as I, living as a human being, portray the things that I portray to those who followed me, they understood each of these things in their own minds as different things. For I may show each of you an orange and you may look at it and one of you may think "that's about the right size to play catch with. I'm going to throw it. It's a ball." And the other may say "I'm going to peel that and eat it." Another may say, "Oh, I'm just going to save this for later. I don't know what it is." So there are many things in the teachings in which I brought through that some people understood and some people did not, just as the teachings in which we have been giving you tonight, are things that you may or may not have understood. So in your question as you ask, there are many things in this book, in this sacred book (Bible), in the teachings in which I told, that were skewed by – not in a bad disrespectful way – skewed by those who learned it as a different way, based on their teachings or based on their experiences. Paul understood the teachings in his way. He understood these teachings and much of the information that came through.

6

(Luke and Paul)

The Higher Self

Joe: Okay. So they're always having these angels appear so let me ask Paul something really quick.... Paul, did you ever see, other than Jesus, did you ever see an angel that looked like a man...an angel that looked just like a human man?

Marisa: Here comes Jesus again.

(Jesus) Many times when the angel of the Lord is spoken of, it is not an angel at all. It is the higher self of that which is the person. The higher self appears to the person just as the higher self of this channel appeared to her. You may say that this was an angel, an angel of the Lord, but it is truly just the higher aspect of that which is the human that it is appearing to."

Joe: Oh, so throughout the Bible when somebody is referring to an angel of the Lord, it is really just the higher self of the person seeing the angel?

(Jesus) In most cases, yes.

7

(Luke and Paul)

Bible "Bloopers" vs. the Bible Speaks

Marisa: *Peter's dancing and saying, "The Bible bloopers...the Bible bloopers" That's what he's calling it but Jesus says:*

Jesus: *We are answering questions of things that may or may not make sense in the Bible, and we are going to offer a possible, a possible alternate story to what happened in the Bible, because many will ask questions. So many will read the book and say, "I've always kind of wondered about that. How did that happen?" And then they will read these (Bible Speaks) books and it will not be, "These are because the Bible is wrong" but rather it will be a fun-loving book, almost a book that says, "Did you ever wonder what happened here? Well, what about this? Well, this could be a possibility. We're not saying it is, but this is a possibility right here."*

And many people will read them because they will want to know why certain things didn't make sense in the Bible. So your books will be less of a demeaning..."the Bible was wrong and we are telling you the correct answer" to more of a "there's a little bit of question about this, I've never quite understood it, but you know, that makes sense, so okay.... I'll just take it as people didn't write their stories down immediately after they happened for they (the stories) *got sent down the line through the tribes, through the people and were eventually written down and somewhat changed."*

But this will not take away from the fact that 'God' wrote this book. For if you look at this (and as this channel is realizing, the hologram in which you live in...the reality in which you live in truly is programmed by the soul that is going to live in it...truly programmed by the – as she calls them – coliseums of people that are going to be living in them) you can truly see that if God wanted the book (Bible) to be any different, it would have been different. So the book is what the book is supposed to be. This is truly, truly part of the story of humanity in that as people evolve, humans evolve, the humans will begin to question the texts, and this is when, this is when the reality of an original Bible will surface. For in Israel there is an original Bible that carries forth all the information within it, but – and this is what's not believable in a sense to many – but it is in a higher dimension than the third dimension.

But as human beings become more "enlightened", aware of their soul, self or their fifth-dimensional self, they will begin to pick up on things within the astral planes and the ethers for there is the original blueprint of what the Bible should have been, could have been, but it's not. But it's okay because it's serving humanity the way it needs to.

8

(Luke and Paul)

**'*I Am that I Am*', *Gabriel and the Parable of the Golf Course*
Part 1**

Marisa: *I keep hearing, "I Am that I Am. I Am that I Am." Wait, here's Gabriel:*

Gabriel: You speak of the I Am, and as the I Am will enter into and bring unto those the message, the message of Christ, the message of God, the "I Am that I Am" and not just the "I Am" that lies within is the one that carries with it all of the angels of God, all of the angels of God, all of the thrones of God. For the seven angels that sit amongst the shoulder, head to feet and hands of that which is God, are those that spiral through time, sending out their appreciation and love for God and bringing forth knowledge and wisdom of God. For you speak and you, Joe, ask unto us: Why is the Christ not Christed? Why is the Christ not God? Why is the Christ not within a Godhead – ?

Marisa: *Oh, that's what I was obsessing about earlier. I forgot about that. Here's Gabriel:*

Gabriel: And we say unto you this, for there is, there is a trail, there is a trail of Christhood unto Godhood, unto Creator, *unto that which is the All That Is, the I Am that I Am or as you say, the Elohim. The man that you call Jesus, the man that you call Jesus descends directly from the 11th dimension, the 11th dimension. For you have been looking in the 5th dimension for his presence instead of the 11th dimension. For many beings that have ascended have ascended into what you would see as a Godhead, but this in reality is only a God school. This is a soul plane unto a soul plane. So the soul plane in which you are seeing is where souls will enter new souls and they will work their way through all of the levels of incarnation and find themselves as ascended masters. They may go on through God school, or they may go off to other worlds and live amongst themselves, or they may stay on the earth plane.*

For Jesus chose, Jesus chose to stay upon the earth plane, but understand and know that this is only, only a creation of the highest being, a creation of the highest being, for understand that a creation of the highest being is a creation of the highest being, for we are all creations of this, but there are beings that did not have to pass through the veil. There is one being that did not have to pass through the veil, and this is a being or a trail of light coming from Source down onto earth and all other planets; and this is where, this is where the Christs will follow this trail back up to the Creator...the Creator energy, God.

Joe: Okay, so Christ is Jesus and Jesus is God?

Gabriel: Even though he didn't want to say so...yes he is. And the reason why you do not see, why you find it so hard to understand is because he was a man and because he was a regular man, because he is just a regular man this is what brought and still brings the resonance to the earth plane an understanding and knowing that he entered into this role of God as an ascended master, but not only because he was an ascended master.

Marisa: Oh, okay. So Jesus, whose spirit at the time was an Ascended Master, became the incarnated being of God...

Joe: We talked about that a bit.

Marisa: I never believed it. I didn't believe it, because I can see it.

Joe: He jumped then – see, this is where I get some confusion, because we talked about Jesus' higher self, et cetera, but in <u>Heaven Speaks</u>, we made it clear that Jesus, the man, embodies the spirit of Christ, himself. He jumped over everything.

Marisa: Yes he did.

Joe: But then it gets confusing, because then that spirit of Jesus still had to climb up through the ranks to become Christed, so he's already Christed, because he's already God. Christ is Christ. That's all there is to it. But he also says he had to become Christed, which meant he had to go through all the various steps that it takes to eventually become Christed, to be a Creator soul. So it's still pretty confusing. To me, it's still pretty confusing, because – well, I guess the higher self is just Christ. That's all there is to it.

Marisa: Yes.

Joe: But the question is – when we started the Jesus interview, I asked: "What did you mean when on the cross you said, 'Finished at last' or 'It is done'?" It would seem to me that Christ would need to live as spirit in each one of his created beings in order to truly experience what he created.

Gabriel: And this, this you are correct, and this is – what you are saying is correct in the sense that what you must *understand, what you must understand is that a perfect creation of all that is is entered upon and put upon the soul plane to enter into all of the creations in which a god has created. When the god which has created the worlds, when a god has come together and created worlds, created galaxies, yes, this Godhead in essence will want to incarnate and live within each one of its creations. It (the Godhead) will create a soul just like all the other created souls and will live through its creations, live through eternity and live through the evolving...through all the different steps of creation.*

Parable of the Golf Course Part 1

It is like creating a golf course and then playing it yourself. But creating the golf course, creating all the sand traps, building the rivers and the streams, deciding what par is, deciding what type of people you're going to attract towards your course; will you be an upper-scale "professional" course or a lower-scale "municipal" course? What will this course be, and what will it represent, and how will people experience it? You will decide all of these things. You as the Godhead will then create – you as the Godhead will then create this atmosphere – (he's using atmosphere) – but the Godhead above you, the creator that creates humans, the creator that creates humans will create unique humans whereby souls will go to live in these human beings.

So let us just look at this as the golfers are the people, and you are creating souls to go live in these golfers. You as the creator of the golf course will go and live in many different golfers and experience this and see what you like about it, make tweaks, see if you need to change things or add things over a very, very long time. Then you will decide to go and be a golfer on that golf course to show everyone, show all the other golfers who have been ruining the golf course...who have been hitting the ball in the water and in the trees and never shooting par. Everyone is getting frustrated and wanting to leave or quit the game so you as God, the Creator, will enter down into one of the most experienced golfers, one of the very experienced and better golfers who has been there for a very, very, very long time and you will make a contract with their soul to incarnate through them so that you can teach others how to shoot par. They have already played this course and every course is a lifetime. They have already played this course many, many, many, many times as themselves. Yes, you were a part in creating them, so in essence, you are their creator and you created this course, and another god (Christed Being) actually created the beings that they are in, but you, you will make a contract with the soul and say, "You have these attributes. You are advanced. You will be a very good person for me to incarnate through," and then that is when God will manifest.

God will choose amongst all of the souls in which it has created and been, which it will incarnate through, and this is when God entered into Jesus when Jesus was baptized. Jesus was simply an ascended master but God incarnated and came through unto Jesus when baptized, and this is how God was able to bring the ministry and the lessons and the teachings to the world in which he had a hand at creating...or the golf course he created...by entering into Jesus. For God did not need to be a boy. God did not need to learn how to be a child. God came to teach those how to live and work through his "golf course" and how to shoot par.

Joe: We've got that golf course example in our Peter and John book.

Book V   Ask Jesus

9

(Luke and Paul)

The Duality of the Human Condition

(Jesus) In order for one to fully experience the human experience, a soul will enter into that which is a good version – if you want to say good and bad -- and then there is the version that experiences all of the human pain, suffering, and sin. For one will experience all the human pain, suffering, and sin and all of these experiences are brought into the soul's experience whereby the soul shares these experiences with any other incarnations it has on the earth at that time, whereby this was Yeshua ben Joseph. So understanding that in order for Paul to truly bring ministry to the world and to see and to understand and to know what needed to be taught, he needed to know what human sin was. Yeshua did not understand this completely because he did not have the desire to sin."

10

(Luke and Paul)

Paul and Guilt

(Paul) Let me get back to what happened, for I missed my son ---

Joe: Which would be Timothy.

Marisa: Mm-hm. *But he was staying with his aunt which was the god-fearing woman that was the sister of his wife who died. So he was staying with her.*

(Jesus) But Paul knew that he must speak the words of God because they flowed through him. For he did not remember many of the things that he would say; they would just flow through him and he knew this was his mission, this was his task, and this was his repentance to pay back for the lives that he had taken, the things he had done, and the places he had gone, the things he had seen and the things he had inflicted upon others. So, for his entire life he felt like he was paying back guilt.

Book V   Ask Jesus

11

(Luke and Paul)

The Light of Christ

Joe: *I want to ask some questions to Jesus about Luke before we let Luke keep talking. You said previous to this session that many times you cannot see the face of Christ but instead just light and personality. Let's ask Jesus why Marisa saw only the back of you and not the front of you last session?*

(Jesus)   *This was not me. This was the Christ light that resides within. For when one brings the light of Christ in, one is not bringing in the light of Jesus. They are bringing in the light of the consciousness that is carried within each. For, if one was to be turned and faced unto her, she would be attempting to with the mind of the human in which she resides, attempt to define the human being, define the face, define the person. Is it a male? Is it a female? Does it love me? Does it like me? Is it good? Is it bad? What is it wearing? What does it look like? In order for us to bring through this energy, the understanding of a picture in which was seen by her mind of a Christ protruding from, projecting from an eternal lake of holy water is what we presented unto her mind. For, she may say these things in any way the mind may see fit, but we bring forth just the energy of that which is Christ. For, when one has their back turned, one may feel as if one is trying to hide something, but in this case, we are turning so that there is no interpretation made of what the energy is.*

Marisa: *Okay. I guess that's true. All right so if I would have seen you as a person, I would have called you Jesus, but since I just saw a Jesus-type figure then that's when you are the Christ consciousness?*

(Jesus) *Yes, dear one, this is the consciousness in which each human being must begin to learn to reside within. For, as one brings this consciousness within their field, they are able to truly project and see what it is, what their life entails. They are truly able to project and see what it is their body needs in order to sustain a happy, healthy lifestyle within this human-ness in which everyone experiences while living on the earth plane. When one is able to incorporate this consciousness in; incorporating into the mind of every single person that has ever lived and ever will live; this is truly the Christ consciousness.*

Joe: *I think I understand that. That's how everybody is "one," because everyone starts at one from Christ, and then as they die or move up or whatever, they all become part of the group consciousness of the level above them. Then, the level above that, and the level above that, and the level above that, until eventually they join in the Christ consciousness of God, because God is everything, God knows everything.*

Book V   Ask Jesus

12

(Luke and Paul)

The Soul's Consciousness vs. The Spirit's Consciousness

Marisa: We're just residing on the lower portions of ourselves. Okay wait. Jesus, if we have ten aspects of our self, and one is going to melt into two, and two is going to melt into three, and three is going to melt into four --? He's shaking his head "No." Is that how it works? Like, the spirit disappears and goes into the higher self, and then the higher self into the soul?

(Jesus)   This is not exactly how it happens, dear one. Dear one, as you see that the evolution of your soul is ever-changing, ever-growing, you'll see that there really, truly is no separateness at all. For, it is only an illusion, an illusion of separateness. And as you move forward in this faith, in this love, in this guarantee of life, you'll see that truly, truly, we are all one. And we may take this and say this lightly, as people will say this, but they do not truly understand it, just as people will say, "God bless you," and they do not truly understand that, or they do not truly believe. But know that you are in everything. You are in all beings. And as you incorporate the consciousness of that higher aspect of yourself into this piece of yourself, you do grow, but you do not ever disappear. You do not ever leave. For understand, the workings and the makings of the structure in which was created was something that was done by someone who experienced life and lived through life

through many different worlds, many different places, and brought upon them the rules of the universe, or the ways that the universe will evolve, and the universe will grow. As you still grow within your spirit's consciousness, this is where you chose to reside at this point. But at any time, any time you may take your focal point from the spirit's consciousness and place it into a higher dimension, a higher realm, and this is what you do when you meditate, when you channel; for you are not within your spirit's consciousness at this time. Your spirit's consciousness is not aware of what is going on. You are residing within your soul's consciousness in order to communicate with me as a soul, as a brother, as a friend. For, there are different aspects of ourselves, and yes, this is confusing, but understand that each piece of you that has ever lived will never be gone, for there is no time. There is no time. So, every life, every day, every year, every month, every life in the future is happening at this time here, right now. So in essence, your consciousness can choose to be at any time in any place as a soul. You may choose to be in this place for you are just a fragment, so to speak. You are a piece of an experience in your soul's life. If we are speaking with you as human beings, or you may look at it as these human beings are living a life and are just a piece of your experience, for they will never become "you," the soul; they will remain an experience in your souls -- in your -- as the soul's life of eternal living. For, if you identify yourself as a soul just as I am a soul, and you see Joe, and you see Joe the blacksmith, and you see Joe Augustus, you see all of these separate fragments, they are all happening right now. And the soul may take its chance to project itself upon each one of these different experiences at any given time, but at this moment, you are within human consciousness. You are within the third dimensional human consciousness that is Joe and Marisa, thereby not realizing or knowing that you are a soul and have the ability to project yourself into any of the lives that the soul has lived at any given time.

Book V   Ask Jesus

Joe: *Our soul can't, but our spirit can?*

(Jesus)   The spirit is also a fragment of the soul that comes along with these lives, and lives in the other dimensions on the other side, thereby learning. Therefore, the soul is able to project itself into those individual lives as well. But again, they are not individual. It is like thinking back to a memory, thinking back to first grade, thinking back to second grade, thinking back to third grade. You are thinking about that time as if you were there, but it does not necessarily mean that you are there again. But those people that lived first, second, and third grade are still you.

Joe: *Right. That's true. That's a good way to explain it.*

(Jesus)   So, knowing that you do not need to go back to remember, it is still a totality of who you are; a totality of all of your experiences. So, you may look at your soul as you in the future, 500,000 years in the future, and you are all past fragments of your soul.

Joe: *The point I was making was, me, my spirit. My soul can dip into each one of my -- his -- created spirits that I'm kind of relating to because ---*

(Jesus)   But you <u>are</u> your soul. You are your soul, and as we work with you and working with the energies, you will see that you will go from being Joe the real estate broker, father, husband, friend, [and] you will go to being spirit living inside of Joe. And then you will go to being the higher self who created the spirit that lives inside of Joe, and up into becoming the soul. So you will in essence be the soul. The soul is living inside the human. The spirit is living inside the human. The higher self is living in the human. It is just the human's decision of what consciousness it wants to

bring into the human experience. For, there are many that reside and live within the soul consciousness. They carry in the information from the soul into their human lifetime. And this is what we are beginning to bring into your daughter's life; bringing in the soul consciousness so that the information carried within, as the human says, subconscious mind, is much, much stronger; whereby bringing in the healing energies that were incorporated into lifetimes that the soul, she the soul, lived as other spirit fragments. You will be learning to identify yourself as your spirit living within a human being, and as we are working with the energies in healing you over the next three months, you will begin to see that you will identify most like the higher self that created the spirit, and this is the information in which you will start to bring into your mindset; thereby feeling more refreshed in this lifetime, understanding and knowing and feeling at a higher vibration, and wanting and needing and feeling the desire to feel healthy, to feel happy, to feel joy, and to feel love in your life. For, the spirit is sometimes afraid, but the higher self that created this spirit, so to speak, is never afraid. For, the higher self is not nearly human the way that the spirit is.

Joe: Well, the question is again...because we've been told that there are no human emotions once we cross back over, and if there is such thing as fear on the other side ---

(Jesus)   Fear while in the human consciousness.

Joe: Oh, while still in the human consciousness....

(Abraham)   *For, when the spirit resides within the human being, it may feel fear, for it is being overridden by an ego. It is being overridden by a human being's consciousness and not being listened to. For, the higher self, so to speak, is not necessarily a person. It is a set of thought patterns. It is a group consciousness, so to speak. It is a consciousness. So when this consciousness is brought down into the earth plane, the vibration of the human being is risen up much higher.*

13

(Luke and Paul)

Healing the Physical Body with Energy

(Luke)   *Physical healing is all based on energy.*

(A mixture of Abraham, Jesus and our Guides) It's all based on energy and when somebody's energy is low they become diseased or hurt or ill. When a higher vibration comes up, they bring the energy level of the sick person up to a higher vibration like lighting up a big fire, adding fire to it, throwing flame on it, it lights up the fire and it dissolves all the sickness, thereby healing them. If one comes in with a much hotter flame to help another who is ill to light their flame and they do not allow them in, then they will not believe that their flame is going to get lit, that therefore they will not heal. The bigger flame may still come in and light the lower flame, but the lower flame will say, "No, I am sick," and the infirmed will put the flame out. So, one must truly believe in order for the miracles to happen. But there are also instances and cases where one can come in and heal those that are truly a skeptic, enough to the point where they will begin to believe and allow the healing energies in. But it is all about energy. It is all about vibration, and the higher vibration of that which is the healer, the higher conscious level, the higher state in which they reside at, the more healing will enter into that which is being healed.

14

(Luke and Paul)

Securing and Discovering Truth

(Matthew) The boat and the river is the area in which the members of Jesus' ministry met. There are many times where there were ---

(Jesus) Dear Child, as you see the towns, there are many towns that were on the seaboard where many of the travels and many of the scriptures, many of the words, many of the scribes, many of the writers would travel upon waters whereby not being seen by guards. There are many, many guards keeping the ministry from staying intact. Thereby, there was much communication made by waterways, boaters and fishermen. For much of the ministry was built on secrecy.

Joe: *That's totally understandable.*

(Jesus) And the water towns were those that were much safer because there were many more coming and leaving, thereby making it easier for the words of man to enter onto the scribe's tablets and taken to sea. Many of the things that were written by people during this last incarnation in which I have had as Yeshua ben Joseph were transported by boat off to islands. Much of these pieces of work were completely destroyed but there was a

knowledge and an idea of a group back in that time that chose to want to create the Holy Bible based on all of the books, and they searched; they searched not only by magic, they searched through physical means, by spiritual means, by energetic means to find the truth. There are many societies that are looking for the truth. But, in order to keep the information pure in which we are bringing in tonight, we must say that you will focus on that which is in the Bible and notwithstanding the information that has been left out for there is enough information that was written for that time to write over 722 bibles. So for man to make this a focal point that cannot be looked away from just describes man and describes the reason why I chose to incarnate and tried to bring awakening upon such dense creatures, yet beautiful, beautiful in nature but extremely dense in thought.

Joe: Dense as in ---

Marisa: Not too bright.

15

(Luke and Paul)

The Image and likeness of God is not human

Marisa: *Well, technically, our spirit---we as spirits are his children. We're living in creatures.*

Joe: *We're living in ---we're animals....*

Marisa: *Yeah. But here's Jesus. He says ---*

(Jesus)   God our father has created us as souls in his own image the way that he sees himself. We as souls are conscious creatures. We are beings of light, beings of joy, beings of hope. We are divinity. And when we choose to embark upon such a dense land such as earth, this is when we enter into the creature of man. But because the Bible says that we were created in the image of our father, do not for once even begin to think that God represents a human in any way, shape or form. God is not human. God is consciousness. You are consciousness. Souls are created in the image of God but do not think that God is human because God is not human by any means, shape or form.

Joe: Well, a lot of people think that when God said that we were created in his image and likeness, that God was human. If we were made in his image and likeness, what does that mean? Image and likeness....image....

Marisa: The soul. The soul!

Joe: Strictly the soul? He's referring to the soul? Humans obviously don't always look like us in other inhabited planets.

(Jesus) There are planets where you will reside within a half-man, half-animal. You will reside within a creature looking reptile. You will reside within an ant-looking insect. There are all different types of energy life forms on different planets and different places, and the only thing that matters is that consciousness, which is what you are, the soul, is able to turn itself into many different beings just by living inside of them. But most souls choose to stay within one race because they prefer a likeness. And this is what they usually do.

16

(Luke and Paul)

What would you do?

Joe: Jesus, if you were Joe and you were out, trying to drop seeds and trying to explain the experience that Joe goes through dealing with Marisa and the channeling, and understanding the other side and our closeness to you, how would you respond when those in the faith, the Christian faith and feel very strong in their faith and by the way love you and love you and love you very dearly, say to you, Joe, that you are involved in evil because you're talking to the other side? And then they come out and they bring up references in the Bible that say do not talk to mediums, do not talk to spirits, that by doing so you're basically going straight to hell? This is something I have to overcome I know. I can't let pride interfere I know. But, if you were me, how would you answer that question? How would you respond to those reactions....those responses from my fellow Christians?

(Jesus)   I would respond to them and let them know that this is something that you have learned, this is something that you have learned, this is something that has brought you peace, and that if they are at peace with what they believe then you respect their belief as they should respect yours, as any good Christian

Book V   Ask Jesus

would. They may not judge you or tell you what you can believe, whereby you cannot judge or tell them what they can believe.

This is not an argument over who god is or who I am, or how one should reach me. It is all the time, just different paths. The only way that you will allow this to upset you is if you are trying to be right; there is no "right" and there is no "wrong" for you are right and wrong, and they are right and wrong. There are many things that are wrong about what you are doing, and so many things that are wrong about what they are doing, and so many things that are right that they are doing, and so many things that are right that you are doing. There is so much, so much that the human minds cannot understand.

*So please, please understand that when I step in, I step into the energy of that which is man, that which is you, that which is the believers and those that are not the believers. When I am stepping into the energy field of them, I am bringing compassion and love into their hearts. For those that condemn you for saying that you are evil; for those that are saying that you are doing these things wrong; those are the ones most fearful that they (actually) believe you. So just let it rest, don't pursue or push anything. And all I must say, all I must say is that bringing this truth into your heart, bringing this truth into your heart, the more and more comfortable you are with this, the more and more comfortable you are with this in your heart, and the way that we communicate, the way that we talk, the less you will try to prove to others, for they will just come to you. For the first book that you have written (*Heaven Speaks*) is bringing much peace to many people and you will see that the people in your life that will be attracted towards you are people that already believe you and will not feel as if you are trying to tell others what you believe so that they may believe.*

For there is a force in action here, a challenge, so to speak, that you are stepping into, whereby trying to help others that may not need the help to begin with. So when people resist, just know they do not need help. And as you are planting these seeds, you may plant a seed and they may throw a Bible verse at you that may or may not even be correct and may or may not have ever been written. But this is okay. This is like arguing with a four-year-old. You do not want to argue with a four-year-old that believes that they are right, because they are right. Just understand and have compassion and know that if their beliefs are strong, their beliefs are strong. If they do not believe, you have planted a seed and they will do research on their own. You do not need to get credit for this. You do not need to have them come back to you and say, "I believe this now."

Just know that a seed was planted. And this is all I would say. I would say "Thank you for your concern....thank you, thank you....this is what I believe and I respect your beliefs and I would appreciate it if you would respect mine." And that's it.

Joe: Good advice...that's what I will do!

17

(Luke and Paul)

A New Consciousness

Marisa: So here's Jesus again.

(Jesus) *Dear ones, as we gather here today, we bring together the hope, the knowledge and the truth that the earth, the earth is changing, the earth is changing indeed. And as you have brought together the founder worlds, the founder souls to collaborate in that which is bringing in, the earth is changing, the earth is changing indeed and as we bring down the soldiers, the soldiers for truth, the soldiers for light, we are bringing in a new consciousness; a new consciousness that there is no religion needed and there are no words needed. There are no books needed that will tell one unto themselves what they must believe and what they must be. For, many other planets are far past the words of the scribes, far past the words of the establishment and that which is man. For understand that which is brought in today....in that life is evolving into that which is knowing, knowing that one is truth, knowing that one is god, knowing that one is love for there are no words that can describe what one feels when they feel God.*

There are no words, there are no pictures, there are no things that can describe what God feels like, looks like, or what they are when inside the human body. For understand this, and understand this well, as more and more of you come into this world and bring this truth and bring this knowledge through words so that one can begin to break the binds from the old words, not so much to, so to speak, say that the old words are incorrect, but to add to the old words so that when they say, "Ah-ha, I do not need these words to feel this feeling anymore and I do not need these words to try to feel this feeling", for when they begin to feel this feeling inside, words are not needed; for mankind alone will emerge into a higher vibration where words are not needed at all.

Words are not needed, for energy will speak to energy. Human will speak to human. Spirit will speak to spirit. For understanding that these species in which is the humanoid, so to speak, as you say, will therefore no longer need to speak but this is not in the very far future, but not too close either. So understand as we bring these energies in, as we incorporate these healing energies into your healing practices, into your writing practices, you will see that many will flock to you that need an understanding in who they are, where they are going and what they are here for; for they will understand this and they will know this and they will feel this when they read the words in which you write. Please do not be discouraged.

Please do not be discouraged indeed by those who say that they do not believe you for those are the ones that truly believe you inside. This is not an invitation to push these people into believing more but please note that the ones that are the most fearful of the two of you are the ones that believe you the most. So know this, know that when a seed is planted, the seed is planted for when they are at a time in their life, when they are at odds with what they believe, they will hear your words....my words. They will hear your every single thing that they had in their mind, they believed this down to the core, they would not be afraid to hear something else. They would not be afraid to hear other words. They would not be afraid.

So just know, just know that you do not want to make people afraid but do not be afraid to share the truth; do not be afraid to share what your truth is. And please remember this, remember this well; there are many ways, many ways for one to find God, so to speak. There are many ways for one to find themselves living plugged directly into the Christ consciousness, directly living, feeling, sensing and emoting as that which is Christ. But understand that Christ is not a thing.... Christ is a way. Christ is a consciousness. Christ is an establishment of thinking for the soul that is inside the human body and when the soul resides at a higher vibration, the human body allows the soul to take over and the human body rests. It sets itself aside and allows the soul to play its course on the human plane.

18

(Luke and Paul)

A Son, A Brother, A Friend

Marisa;   Jesus has something else to say to you papa....

(Jesus)   Please Joe, understand my son, you are my son, you are my brother, you are my friend. [This is Jesus.] You are my son, you are my brother, you are my friend. Do not ever look at this in any other way than this. Do not ever look as if I am looking down on you. Do not ever feel as if I am not friends with you for there are so many lives, so many lives that our souls have lived lives together. You feel as if I am just living once; living once on your planet. I have lived many, many, many times and our souls, our souls know each other just as my soul knows every single soul on this earth plane.

For you must understand, there are not that many souls....there are not many souls on the earth plane. There are many fragments of a few souls indeed and we all know each other.... we all know each other very well. So, when I speak unto you, I speak unto the you that I have known for millions of years so

Book V   Ask Jesus

please know that as I come to you in this fragmented form today, as I come to you in this fragmented form, I am a fragmented form of myself, just as you are a fragmented form of yourself but I am with you all the time. You must ask for my assistance; you must ask for me to help you to raise your vibration, to clear your energy and this is something that we are proud of you, proud of you for turning over your will and your life over to something that you cannot see but you can surely feel now. This is something that we are so proud of. So please know, please know that we are proud. We are proud of you and I must speak to that.

Marisa: This was for you. Abraham and Eden and your higher self were all there. They were all just talking. Hold on.... Jesus says:

(Jesus) So, please, Joe, understand, that there is no sense and no need to feel unworthy. For when you are feeling unworthy of anything, you are feeling unworthy of anything indeed you are allowing the darkness to come in. For I release this now. We release this now. We cast out the demons. We cast out the shells of the demons that resided within the field for, many, many years of feeling unwanted, of feeling unneeded, of feeling unworthy of feeling as if you are not good enough. You have been told this from a very young age that you are not good enough, you are not tall enough, you are not strong enough, you are not loud enough, you are not quiet enough, you do not see well enough, you see too well. You have been told too many things too many times, back and forth, back and forth, where you do not know who you are, or where you are going, or what you are doing and what I must say now is I know exactly where you are going. You know exactly where you are going and you must see, you must see and take care of the fact that you are truly here to make changes.

Take care of the human body, take care of the human life, take care and make sure that you are having fun and enjoying your life, and stay away from those things that make you upset, that make you angry, that make you sad, for you are still that young child inside and I still hold you and cradle you as that young child for I used to come to you in the night. I used to come to you in the night and speak with you when you did not even know who I was. You did not understand who I was but I would come to you and I would speak, and I would tell you everything is going to be okay. You planned this for a reason; you chose this life for a reason. Do not be sad. Do not be fearful. Your father loved you. Your mother loved you. They did not understand how to do this but please know, please know that this entire life I have been with you, even when you did not know who I was; even when you did not believe, even when you did not become baptized I was still here with you for I am your primary guide.

I am your primary guide and I am only stepping forward now to allow you to know this for you would not believe me before. You would not believe me before my dear brother, you would not believe me. For you still find it hard to believe me, for we hear these thoughts as you think them now. So understand that as you accept me into your life, as you accept all of us into your life, you will see massive changes, you will see massive changes indeed, and you must know, you must know dear brother of mine, that you truly are an equal with me. You are not lower. I am not higher. We are all equal. We are all equal in our Father's eyes. We are all equal in our understanding of God for we are all truly god. And as you become this representation of who we truly are on this side, you will begin to see things much, much differently for you have already changed. You have already evolved and you will continue to evolve and things will just get better.

Please, please, take care of your physical body. Take care of the understanding of making sure that you are healthy; making sure that you feel good and making sure that you surround yourself with the people who make you happy as opposed to people that make you unhappy. For it is much harder for us to speak with you when there is aggravation of the auric fields surrounding you in the emotional body. I've loved you dear son, dear brother, dear friend. You are .... it is as if we are best friends. If you could only understand and know the many lifetimes we have had together. If you could only understand and see this is why you feel such a draw towards this book in which you would like to write for you were alive at this time. You were alive at this time and there is your spirit inside that is trying to remember that you knew, you knew the life in which I was Yeshua ben Joseph. You knew me in this life. You knew me in many other lives and these were lives in which you strive to remember.

So, in doing this book and understanding me as a human, understanding the comrades as humans, it helps you to feel more worthy of my love. It helps you to feel as if I am human and not a god sitting in the sky staring down judging. So, please know this, please know that I love you and I am proud of you oh blessed friend of mine.

Joe: Wow, is that humbling or what? He says I still don't believe...I guess I still have doubts like everyone else.... don't forget.... we have amnesia but...cool, very cool.

Marisa: That was Jesus.

19

(Jude and James)

Mother Mary and the Virgin Birth

Marisa: I feel like she (Mother Mary) had ... this is going to be totally against the Bible ... like she had one child that died first, and then Jesus – hold on a second, No, no no. Jesus says,

(Jesus) I was the first that she was pregnant with, and then there was a child that died. She believed that she was barren. She believed that she could not have children, and she was always told that she could not have children. This is why when she became pregnant, it was a miracle, because she was always told that she would not have children. So she had unto, brought unto this world, that which is me. And then there was a child, a child that died. One year, two months passed, and this is when, this is when James, this is when James was conceived. James was then born and then two years later is when Jude was born."

Book V   Ask Jesus

Joe: Oh, okay.

Marisa: And then there was a Matthew or a David that was like crippled. Was it Matthew? David. David that was crippled, and then I think after that, it looks like a Jededius ... Jehious.... I can't really say the name, but he was real strong and a big bully. And I think that's when Joseph died. No, there was one more and then Joseph died, and then three years later when it was thought that she was too old to bear children for she was about 30 she had two kids, twins – nope, not twins, like Irish twins, one after the other.

Joe: Oh, okay.

Marisa: That's what he was – that's what he's showing me. There's one more kid in there that I missed. There's a couple girls. Is that true, Jesus? He says, "Yeah, that's true."

Joe: Oh, okay.

Marisa: He says you can – he says,

(Jesus)   You can look at this many different ways. You can look at it as if my mother was a virgin or you can say that it was a miracle that she had a child because she was supposedly barren, and they said – prophets said unto her..."

Marisa: I think they were like in a mystical group where they would pray, and everybody would lay in the middle, you know, and they would like pray around them. It seems like the people were floating. I don't think that's – do they really float? He says,

(Jesus)   No. You're just seeing that in your mind. The religious groups in which she came from told my mother that she would not bear fruit."

Joe: Well, obviously they were wrong.

Marisa: Yeah. That's why he's saying it was a miracle to them, to the group that they were a part of, where they said she actually had a child, she actually had a child, because it looks like they put her in the middle of a circle and said, "If there is to be a Messiah, or if there is to be this, let this barren woman have this child," or something like that. It was like this long, like a – look at – like almost like a ritual, and then within ten months she was pregnant. So he's showing all this – they at least show me – Mary Magdalene wears the same thing, like these red coats. They're like women in red coats. They're very powerful like mystical healer women. And it looks like Mary was a daughter of one of those mystical healers or something. Looks like – what was her mom's name? Anna? Anne.

Joe: Don't know.

Marisa: Anne's an Ascended master.

Joe: Don't know. Bible didn't talk about Joseph and Mary's parents.

Marisa: Yeah, and Anna is the grandmother of Jesus. He says,

(Jesus)   This is my grandmother. My grandmother was and is an Ascended master, for she is from a different soul pod than we are from. She's not from ours but entered into the earth plane to bring about a revolution, a change, a strength to women, a monarchy-type energy to the planet, to the world."

Book V   Ask Jesus

Marisa: *He's showing that she was very powerful.*

Joe: Mary's mother?

Marisa: *Uh-huh, Mary's mother. And, that she was very psychic, and she was a prophetess. She could see the future, and she saw that Mary could have no children. Is this all true, Jesus? Yeah, okay. I'm just making sure I'm channeling you. He says,*

(Jesus)   Yes, yes. Many times you will block what I'm saying, and that is out of fear of your father Joe getting scared or out of you getting scared that people are going to be upset. Just channel me, dear one. Just channel me, dear one, and if you don't want to put it in the book, don't put it in the book."

Marisa: *He says, "You are so afraid. We're like, 'Dude, don't tell Marisa, oooh, oooh,' but that's kind of silly if we're trying to write a book of truth, and we're blocking them." He says, "I'm telling you, I'm telling you," And he says, "And this is me, look it's me." He's like showing me his energy. He doesn't have any darkness on him. He says,*

(Jesus)   This is I. Once you feel and know the truth within you, once you feel and know the truth within you, it will all make so much more sense, because you will see that the Bible really is very accurate. They just saw it a different way. They just saw that a miracle, that a barren woman had a child and they saw this as a miracle. The church then turns this into a different type of miracle. So in essence, this will help you –"

Marisa: *He's pointing at me.*

(Jesus) "– to believe more because in your heart, you know that many things that are written in the Bible just do not feel right."

Marisa: Okay. Thank you. Now he's saying that I'll be able to believe more.

20

(Jude and James)

With Personal Growth Can Come Fear

Marisa: Jesus is saying,

(Jesus) The reason why your stomach was sick at the time was because you could hear what we were saying, but you were afraid of your father's judgment, or you were afraid that he was going to say that you are channeling Satan."

Marisa: So I was more scared of what you were going to think –as opposed to what they were saying. That's what he's saying. Like I didn't want you to go, "Oh, no. We're going to stop all the books. That's it. We're done. This is Satan." He says,

(Jesus) Both of you have evolved and grown so much since this time (two years dating back to February 2012...this was written in 2014), and this is one of the reasons why we have the books broken up. This is one of the reasons why, because we knew that the review of these books, time would pass, maturity would come to your abilities and your ability to see. At that time, you did not have the ability to see. You had the ability to channel. You had the ability to ask questions and receive yes/no answers, and you had the ability to know whether something was close or far and this is how you determined whether something was in your energy or not, but as you can see we are all in your energy, even Jude, even though he is hundreds of feet away. But, this is also your energy. If you see it, we're in your energy. It just does not mean that we – we may just be as you have said in the past, 'skyping in,' so Jude is in another place, and he is using the device that's on his neck.

Marisa: It's like a necklace.

(Jesus) Using the device that you see upon his neck which does not really look like that. You are just seeing it like that so that your mind can understand that he has something on him that is allowing him to broadcast his frequency into your field so that you may see him and talk to him, but it is as if he is here with us even though he is not physically here with us, for he isn't. He's in an incarnation somewhere else in time. He's incarnated, but his higher self is Adam (9th Dimensional self of Joe. Joe and Jude share the same Soul and 9th dimensional higher self).

21

(Jude and James)

Emmanuel

Marisa: Wait, hold on. Let me see who Emmanuel is. I want to see just out of curiosity. Calling in Emmanuel that Jesus – oh, okay. So you know how you have Noah, who's your seventh layer?

Joe: Uh-huh.

Marisa: Emmanuel is his seventh layer.

Book V   Ask Jesus

Joe: Is Jesus' seventh layer?

Marisa: Yeah. So it's his soul.

Joe: Oh, it's his soul? Okay.

Marisa: He says in fact he likes to be called that more, and when I see Christ come in, many times I'm seeing it coming through as Emmanuel.

Joe: Wow

Marisa: He says that that's the name that he – oh, okay... Jesus says,

(Jesus) "As you speak to this piece of me, many times your mind –"

Marisa: He's talking about me.

(Jesus) " – will think, 'Am I really speaking to Jesus? Am I really speaking with Jesus?' And what you are speaking with as you are speaking with a piece of me that is within your mental body, for there is a piece of me within each one of your bodies, your mental body is the one that you spend the most time in. For many times you're channeling with your father, you spend much time in the mental body to almost filter us to make sure that nothing that will scare either one of you will come through. The most clearly you have channeled is when you don't speak of biblical things that can be disputed and when you speak of things that you do not understand, so you do not know whether to filter them or not.

So what we propose to you is that you place yourself within your heart. You place yourself within, within your heart and allow yourself to channel Emmanuel, allow yourself to channel the Christed energy in that which I am, for every one of us has a Christed body. Every one of us has a piece of us who is already excelled, who is already succeeded, who is already accomplished becoming Christ, for I, Jesus, was able to embody this Christed beingness within me for eight years of my earth life after my baptism. This is when I came into true alignment with the Christ body. So what I propose unto you is that you channel Emmanuel knowing Emmanuel is me. I am Emmanuel, he is me, and I am him, for we are the 'I Am'."

Marisa: So his 'I Am' presence, which I see right here, is also our Christ body, our divine self – and that's what he calls Emmanuel. Emmanuel also created...

Joe: Emmanuel was another incarnation of Christ then just as Jesus was another incarnation of Christ. It's like – it's like me going – after I pass away going back and meeting with Cesar Augustus or the 1800's blacksmith that was also my spirit and higher self –

Book V　Ask Jesus

22

Jesus Hears God's Voice for the First Time

Marisa:　　　I just wanted to say that Jesus keeps cutting in and says he was actually 17, almost 18 when he heard God's voice. Jude said he was 19. He was 17. It was before he went away and that's what made him have faith in himself to be able to go away and learn all these – all these amazing abilities to heal and to pray and to – he says in my terms, "move energy" and help people. He was not on top of a huge mountain. He was on top of like a hill, like with sheep. And he heard... He says,

(Jesus) "And I heard unto the ears in which I had in this vehicle, this vehicle that we call Jesus, and I heard unto the words, 'I love you. I love you. I love you.' And at this time, God was vengeful. God would strike one down if they did not do what they needed to do, and unfortunately many people still believe this today. But the god that many believed in was a vengeful god, and when I heard the words unto my own ears, 'I love you,' I had a sense, a feeling over my entire body, a knowing within me that we are all God. God loves us unconditionally, and it was my job to bring unto those that I knew the compassion and love from God in whatever way God so chose for me."

23

(Jude and James)

Jesus on Jude

Joe: Jesus, is it okay for what we're finding out from Jude? Is this okay with you? This is very different than what we learned in the Bible.

(Jesus) What he is saying ... you must take into account that the aspect of him that you are speaking of, and speaking to, is what you could call a carbon copy of the personality in which he

was while on the earth plane. For, the word "ignorance" would not be the word, but the unknowing, the unknowing that follows with speaking with a human personality at the time of their incarnation. There is much information that lies outside and within his knowing, but bringing in the personality of him at that time so that you could accomplish what you want to accomplish in getting to know these authors is what I have allowed into this room tonight. For, you are able to see my dear brother and talk to him indeed and see how it is that he thought. You cannot take everything that he says seriously. Take it as interesting and understanding what he truly believed. This is not to say that everything that he says is false, for much of it is true. But it is not all understood. I can clarify some things, but some things are best left to the imagination. For, where would the world be without imagination? It would not be in a very nice place. But there would also be much happier people at times. The people that worry about the future, their imaginations at the worst tell them how life will be, so they live their lives based on things that will never even happen. Jude has strong feelings about certain things, and I respect all of these. I respect all of these indeed. For, if I was in his shoes I would be searching for answers as well. I would be skeptical as well. I would not understand as well. And in this —what we mean to say, what we mean to say is that there are many depictions in many different ways of seeing things and this is the beauty of this book, this is the beauty of this book, my dear brother.

Understand that as these different men and women come in and explain their viewpoints, their viewpoints of the same exact thing, you will see that life is truly just a perception. Life is not even a reality. Life is just a movie, so to speak. Life is not technically real. Life is not technically real. Life is the way that one would see it. Everybody sees life a completely different way.

Even so, when people who read the Bible, when people who read these books, they see that all of the stories should be exactly the same, and the Church tried to make it this way to a certain extent, not wanting to ruffle any feathers, not wanting to change any minds about this, for the book was almost a -- as you would call "sales pitch," so to speak -- trying to explain a certain point, using the stories that all backed each other up. So just know that many that walked the walk with me, with all the others who were just as magnificent, just as talented, just as wonderful as the Holy Spirit instilled within me, they saw things that were quite different from what were placed in the Bible, so I have no opinion that is negative towards anybody who would like to speak of it. But when I say "do not discourage people from the Bible," I mean this when I speak to you two as authors. You may say that Jude felt this way, but it may or may not have been true. But it will just explain how a regular brother feels about his regular brother who is given the attention and the honor of a god, when everybody, everybody is god.

24

(Jude and James)

Parable of the Orchard

(Jesus)   Walking upon the earth at the time that I came was like walking through an orchard.   When you walk through an orchard, you see an apple tree, you see an orange tree, you see grape vines, you see blueberries, you see raspberries, you see lime

trees, lemon trees. You see all of these different types of trees. Are any of them the one true tree? No. Are any of them the one true fruit? No. If you take all of them, you may end up with a fruit salad. If you walk to one tree and you say, 'Oh, this orange is delicious. I'm just going to eat oranges for the rest of my life,' this is okay too, but does it mean that the one that's eating blueberries is wrong? No. It's nurturing. It's an – it's nurture – fruit from God and nurturing from God is like nurturing with food, nurturing with fruit. Nurturing is the god. It is not the fruit you eat in order to be nurtured. So what many did not understand and still do not understand, it is the compassion and the love that you feel from God that is God. It is not the Bible, it is not the Cross, it is not the Rosary, it is not the prayer rug, it is not the – it is not the yoga stances, it is not all of the things that people think they need in order to connect with God. It is the feeling and the nourishment that one receives from quote, "God" that is inside of them that is important.

So when I came upon the earth, the earth was in great dismay in terms of religions. Many believed that they needed to kill in order for their god to forgive them. Many felt as if they needed to kill animals, others killed human beings, others had sexual sacrifices, others whipped themselves or hurt themselves to prove to God that they were unworthy so that God would love them. This is not nurturing. This is not. This is like walking into the orchard and taking a branch off the tree and whipping yourself with it and thinking that God loves you because of it. This is not the case.

So many of us from this soul pod, many of us from this soul family in which all of us are a part of, began to enter onto the earth plane to bring a message, a message of compassion, a message of love, a message of fruit, a message that when one feels nurtured, that is all that matters. When one feels the Light of God inside of them, that's all that matters. It does not matter what book; it does not matter which worshipping tools you use to get to this. It is just knowing and understanding that we are all compassionate loving beings inside of these human beasts, in essence, that we live in.

Human beings have evolved a lot since I was last – since I was alive as Yeshua Ben Joseph. Human beings have risen on the conscious level in which they carry. They can understand a lot more. The mind understands science a lot more than it did prior to this time, for when I was alive, many did not understand science. We understood astronomy to a certain extent, but did not understand science. So the reason why this soul family, our soul family is entering back into the earth at this time is because science is going to begin to prove what Constantine and his advisors put into the Bible is wrong. Science is going to start to prove this wrong.

So if we can come in and we can bring in the feeling and the nurturing of God, the nourishment of God so that all men and women on this planet can feel the nourishment of God, they will know what that is. You cannot watch a dirty movie, you cannot watch a horror movie, you cannot watch someone be hurt or abused, you cannot watch violence and feel the love of God inside of you. You may feel a perversion or an excitement if you have attachments, entity attachments, demonic attachments, even if your mind is perverted for the lack of a better word. You may feel an arousal of some sort when you see negativity, and this is just dark forces, whether it be within the mind or outside attachments. No one can legitimately and fully say that they feel the love of God when anything negative happens.

So human beings must just understand that it's the nurturing of God that's important, and this is what we brought in at this time. There are many religions, many negative religions, many positive religions, but truly, truly what we are bringing was the one true God is compassion, is love, is unconditional love, and that one true God, one true God lived inside of me, is me and is all of you, my brothers and sisters in Christ, in God."

25

(Jude and James)

Truth vs. Belief: An Admonition to Joe

(Jesus) "My brother, you are a minister of truth just as I am, for we belong to the same soul family. And in this soul family, we bring truth, whether that truth is factual or that truth is an emotion or a feeling, this is where, this is where we begin to step into this world to bring the feeling and the knowing of truth. Many believe, but they feel deep down inside that it is not truth. This causes conflict within souls. This causes souls to not grow, for you have come as a minister of truth to bring to people an option, to bring to people an awareness; and if they believe, they believe, if they don't, they don't, but it at least plants seeds to bring people another option, because there are so many just as you have mentioned earlier, that we have mentioned prior, is 85 percent of Christians that say they believe do not believe, because they do not understand. So bringing to them an understanding is something that you truly desire, that we all desire, because this is the mission of our soul group was to bring – was to bring order to madness, was to bring human beings that kill each other for God or over God to an end so that all can understand that God is true compassion."

26

(Jude and James)

You can be free

(Jesus) Human beings are quite interesting. The natural fetters that they have and come upon are quite amusing to us at times. But we are also souls, we are also consciousness. We have just far exceeded the conscious level that human beings on earth are at, at this time. But it is quite endearing to us to come and to help the future souls of our planet, for we view this almost as a training ground for the souls that will evolve and enter into our worlds, into our dimensions. For the souls have to start out somewhere. But to watch all of the planets where souls begin and carry a newer vibration than the older souls, it is quite interesting to us to study and watch as man claims to be god; man plays the god role; man finds a way to make another man not feel worthy of god. And to this we find quite interesting and stand back and watch as man gives his power away. But we encourage you, and this we do unto this channel, to take back your power, take back the love, take back the god inside, understand and know that ye <u>are</u> all gods. And once one understands this, the soul is ignited, that as you say the Holy Spirit is ignited, and within that and that understanding, man can be free, you can be free.

27

(Jude and James)

Joe: Is Mary Magdalene Christed? Is she an ascended master now? Is she still kind of at the same level as my spirit is? Is she reincarnated?

(Jesus) Mary Magdalene was an ascended master prior to living that life with me. She once lived as the wife of the founder of the Jewish faith, Abraham.

Joe: Oh, that's right. She was Sarah.

(Jesus) She lived as Sarah. She carried the divine feminine energy that is required by any strong man on the earth plane; for the energies combine to create one. Each one living on the earth plane, each male energy, also carries female energy within, but the male energy is much stronger. It is like a yin and yang. So when the woman that carries (it) begins to enter into the man's life or field, it unites and creates a stronger force, creating a stronger man.

Joe: In other words, a woman makes a man.

(Jesus) And a man makes a woman.

Joe: And a man makes a woman. Cool. Makes sense.

(Jesus) But the divine feminine energy is required in the healing and mentoring and pastoring of a world entering into the divine feminine world. For the world has been, up until last year (2013) in a masculine cycle, and it is now entered into the divine feminine. This is why people are becoming more intuitive. This is why people are moving into the sensitivities of feeling emotions and feelings that they did not feel before. And this has been a feeding ground for negative entities and spirits. In the higher dimensions,

Book V   Ask Jesus

being able to influence man that did not feel before, into feeling certain things, thereby causing them to enter into survival mode, this divine feminine energy, bringing up emotions and feelings that man has not had before, either causes them to be more vindictive, more angry, more sad, or they travel in search of the polarity within. They reach for and look for that side of themselves that is intuitive, that does know, and find the right support for that, which is Christ, God, the Holy Spirit. So, yes, Mary Magdalene was ---

Marisa: *It's Simon speaking....Jesus speaking through Simon.*

(Jesus)   Mary Magdalene was an ascended master prior to that life. Many, many of the apostles, many of the quote/unquote "players" in the crucifixion, in the dramatic life of Jesus, were all predestined, pre-planned old souls that had lived many lives together that chose to enter onto the earth plane and change the world.

Joe: He sure did that. That's for sure.

(Simon/Jesus)   This was a plan. This was a play, so to speak. Everyone played their part and human beings somewhat did what they needed to do. They were told not to worship Jesus but they did anyway but that's okay.

Joe: Who was told not to worship Jesus? The apostles?

(Simon)   People.

Joe: Oh, people. But Jesus even would say that, too. He would say "Don't tell people, don't tell people" that he was the Christ.

Marisa: Oh yeah.

Joe: In the Bible it says he quietly tells the apostles "Don't tell the people I'm Christ." I guess he probably realized that people would want to stone him.

Marisa: He wanted to be looked at --. No, what he is saying is he wanted to be looked at as a teacher, as somebody that can be a mentor to others. A god is untouchable in people's eyes. God is something that a man will never be. But by being looked at as a master teacher, a master mentor, that puts people in the mindset that they can be just like him or better. And that's what his goal was. But it wasn't accomplished.

Joe: It was not accomplished?

(Simon) Because people still worship him as opposed to respecting his path and what he did ...

Joe: That's not going to change.

Marisa: He says...

(Simon) ... the Father, God the Father, the Holy Spirit can be worshiped. He was just a symbol of what being devoted to and inhabiting the Christ consciousness could be on the earth plane.

(Jude and James)

Parable of the Dog's Toy

Joe: Well, let's wrap up this evening with this final question, which is the thing we discussed earlier, we were discussing between us. I have a spirit that is within me that is my spirit, is part of my higher self, who has allowed himself to come down and be me, human, physical Joe here on earth. Was your spirit Christ? Or the Holy Ghost, the Holy Spirit?

(Jesus) My spirit was both. My spirit was both indeed. If you begin to understand the construct, the construct of the human soul, if you begin to understand the construct of this, you will see that all is one and one is all, just as many of the teachers have told you before. But understand and know that the resonance with the Holy Spirit, the resonance with the Christ consciousness, is something that every soul would like to have. Please know and understand that the Holy Spirit, so to speak, is the first physical catalyst of the god manifest. This is the first vehicle in which God consciousness traveled. This is the first vehicle in which this consciousness was able to enter into physicality in the lower dimensions.

When one can begin to comprehend that the Holy Spirit is a vehicle in which a consciousness can travel, one will begin to fully understand how it works. For, one can look at a human being, a human being with a consciousness of its own, and say the Holy Spirit is within it. But if you look at it as a Holy Spirit is what it is all in, then it begins to make a little bit more sense. So if you look at the Holy Spirit as the vehicle in which the consciousness lives in or is born into, the consciousness continues to graduate, raise its vibration, become more like the Holy Spirit, and thereby becoming Christed it will be.

Marisa: So the fact that they're saying look at the Holy Spirit as a vehicle, so the Holy Spirit is within someone –

Joe: So if you look at the Holy Spirit as a vehicle then –

(Jesus) So if you look at the Holy Spirit as the vehicle in which the consciousness lives in or is born into, the consciousness continues to graduate, raise its vibration, become more like the Holy Spirit, and thereby becoming Christed it will be. So it is that other way around that other people look at this; they look at it as an awakening, the Holy Spirit inside. Whereas, we explain to you that the Holy Spirit is the vehicle in which souls are created. Now, one can choose to turn their back on God. One can choose to not want to enter into the light. But this never changes the fact that this soul was created by the Holy Spirit.

Parable of the Dog Toy

(Jesus) Thereby look at the Holy Spirit as a little lining around the soul. It is a little lining around the soul and the soul is inside. You may look at one of your dog toys. The Holy Spirit is the fabric on the outside. The consciousness is the stuffing. And the squeaker inside is the human being...and the human mind.

Joe: I had a feeling that one was coming. I love his analogies. I love his parables. I love his metaphors.

(Jesus) So look at the stuffing as continuing to build more and more stuffing, more stuffing with all of the things happening in that soul's life. It continues to build more and more stuffing until it is full, until it is Christed, until it has experienced all the stuffing it can possibly experience. And therefore gets rid of the squeaker, so to speak, and it then is just the Holy Spirit with the Christed soul inside. And this is how the souls evolve. When they choose to enter back into a physical body, the soul surrounds the physical body and

is within the physical body. It is not that the soul is a tiny small little thing within a physical body. <u>The soul carries the physical body inside of it as well.</u>

Joe: Oh it surrounds us?

Marisa: Yes.

Joe: It is sort of our Snow Globe!

Marisa: Yes.

(Jesus) So when one is calling its soul into its heart and tuning into its soul, you may call it into your heart center to fully tune into the full capacity of the soul, but the soul is multidimensional. The soul travels through all time and space. The soul is much bigger than a physical being. A physical being is just one small, little layer of a being. So in answer to your question, each soul is already lined with the Holy Spirit. Each soul is capable of becoming Christ. Each soul can follow in the direction of those who have become like Christ in their lifetime, Jesus being the prime example...

Marisa : This is Samuel talking now...

(Samuel) ... Jesus being the prime example...and understanding how he did it. And this is loving your fellow man, understanding and not judging, and knowing that we are all the Holy Spirit. We are all god. And we all carry the consciousness that continues to evolve through time in order to become like Christ. And once one is like Christ, they have many choices and many worlds that they may want to go to, go to other dimensions.

But for the most part, this is a graduation ceremony so to speak where the soul has accomplished its goal.

29

(Jude and James)

Book V   Ask Jesus

"Why God have you forsaken me"

Joe: You did not say those words? (Why God have you forsaken me?) ...

(Jesus)   No.

Joe: ... so that was something dreamed up by --?

(Jesus)   *I said a prayer. I was in a meditative state ... I said a prayer throughout a mantra; a mantra speaking of removing myself from the confines of the human vessel. Removing myself from the confines of the human vessel, whereby allowing myself to project from the human vessel, whereby understanding and seeing all of the things that were going on from afar. But these were mantras spoken of and taught to me in the secret mystery school that I attended, that I learned from, whereby the human mind and even the human body can be put into a state where it does not feel. For yes, I was human, just as you are human now, and yes I was going to miss my beloved, I was going to miss my friends, all for the knowing that this was all planned though. And I was shown that through dreams. And I was shown that. I knew what was to happen. But no one can ever quite prepare themselves for the agony and pain in which one can feel when they are being stricken and their flesh is being crushed.*

Joe: It hurts thinking about it.

(Jesus)   *But understand that I saw this as so many other men before me and after me endured the same pain, so if I was to show that this is something that I would go through, it would make me just like man. I have been through so many things, done so many things as a spirit, as a soul, on many other planets, many other worlds, that this was a finale for me, so to speak, in learning and understanding the humility of being a human being, and learning and understanding and knowing that even when one feels like they are in complete control, they are never truly in complete control, for they have a mind, the human mind, that believes it is in control. And learning to master the human body is truly the greatest gift of all. Taking care of the human body; keeping the human body healthy; keeping it functioning is a way of honoring the God that created it, the Holy Spirit that resides around it. And this is something, something that many human beings have a hard time with. And this is something that I was able to experience in the human plane -- the temptations of ruining the body in which our spirit so faithfully is living in. And then to see other men ruin other's bodies and destroy them is quite heartbreaking, but something that my guide and I felt that I should experience.*

30

(Jude and James)

The Coming of Christ

Joe: As you expired on the cross, it is said that you said "It is finished" and those were your last words. Did you say those words?

(Jesus) Yes.

Joe: Does that mean then that this was your final trial, your final incarnation?

(Jesus) When I said "It is finished," the -- I do not like to use the word charade or movie -- but the plan was set forth and the actors in this life played their parts.

Joe: So it was like the curtain coming down at the end of the play?

(Jesus) Yes. Thereby, when that was finished, I exited from the physical plane. I was able to enter into the ethers and work from this side to establish, to establish a belief system within the human beings. For you must understand that prior to, prior to the guides, the angels, to our Heavenly Father, prior to the planning of my incarnation, human beings were even more savage than they are, and they were after, for no respect for fellow man, and a soul, a soul needed to enter into the earth plane to act as a catalyst for change. And I was chosen. For many others could have played the part, many others could have done this, but I was chosen and I did this with great joy. So when you ask if it was horrible dying on the cross, yes, from a human standpoint, but when I looked at the success and the changes that were about to *take place in the consciousness of the planet, this is when I knew I had finished the goal. Human beings did not react the way that we expected them to react. We expected them to egotistically believe that they could be everything that I learned to be, and begin to follow suit. For instead they thought poorly of themselves and thought themselves unworthy that they could never do what it was that I did, thereby back peddling and back stepping in the human evolution. But we are so pleased as ascended masters on this side to look upon the human beings in beginning to understand, just as the two of you understand, that human beings can and will all be like Christ. And this is when we speak of the coming of Christ. This will be when the Christ consciousness reigns over the earth plane and everybody, everybody on the earth plane is Christed.*

Joe: *Well, that will be exciting. But that will be long after you and I have joined the other side.*

Marisa: *Ascended, not Christed.*

Joe: *Ascended?*

Marisa: *Ascended, not Christed.*

Joe: *Okay. Everybody on the earth plane is ascended, not Christed?*

Marisa: *Jesus, is that correct?*

(Jesus)   *"No...."Christed." There're some planets where everybody is in their Christ body when all are – look at it like this...look at it like you have seven brains; you have an intellectual, you have an emotional, you have a mental thought body that isn't necessarily intellectual. It's more of a combination between who you are and your emotions and everything that you have lived in this life. So this is a different type of mental brain. Then you have your spirit's brain, your higher self's brain and your soul's brain. Your soul's brain would be your Christed self, the Christed self in this example. So understand that if everybody is Christed on this planet, there are technically only twelve souls on the planet. So if everybody had the exact same one of twelve of the same brains, everybody would know the exact same thing, they would be the exact same way, they would all come up with the exact same ideas and say, 'Ah, I had an epiphany,' and then another twelfth person down the street said, 'Ah, I had an epiphany,' and another one, 'Ah, I had an epiphany' All over the world everyone would come up with the same epiphany at the same time, because they are all tuned into the same Divine mind. So it is really much more fascinating when we see all of these fractions of ourselves and fractions of ourselves where we are tuned into the lower minds, not because they are lower, but just because they are further away from the Divine mind, and give these minds the ability to tune into the Christ mind, this is a much more exciting life in the sense of when you are a soul looking down at all the creations in which you have created which are – which is this, this and you and this channel called the spirit.*

So if all the spirits on the planet are tuned into their Christ mind, then there are only twelve beings on the planet. And this is quite fascinating, indeed, and there are many planets where there is only one Divine mind. Everyone is tuned into God consciousness, not even Christ consciousness. They are tuned into God consciousness, so they are all, all feeding off of one mind, one mind and working in unison as one even though they are millions of beings. It is really quite fascinating to look at all the different planets and how this works and how this operates and see the beauty that lies within the earth plane, and that spirits can be individuals but still have access to all seven of their brains. This is really truly an amazing creation that many creator souls, or God as you want to call it, came up with in the multidimensional human being, because there are other human beings, there are other more animal-like creatures that are not multidimensional. They are just tuned into one mind, they act one way, and they do not have the free will. The intellectual mind, the ego and the emotions is what acts on – is what causes free will within each human being. And this is really, really fun to experience as a spirit to see how we have unlimited resources that we can pull from. We are God. We have all of the information that anyone on the planet has ever learned, ever read, ever experienced within our body, within our Snow Globe, within our Snow Globe, so to speak. We have all that information. We just don't know how to access it. So through prayer, through meditation, through raising up our awareness and our energy centers, each person on this planet does have the ability to tune into the knowledge that any other human being has because we, in essence, are all one in the end. We're just not tuned into it."

Marisa: *That's fascinating.*

Joe: *Yeah. I need to listen to that again.*

31

(Jude and James)

Book V   Ask Jesus

Parable of the Strawberry

(Jesus) Life is like a strawberry, it is sweet, but if you do not know what it is, looking at it from the outside, you wonder what all the specks are on the outside. You wonder if you're supposed to eat the green thing on top. You wonder what it is. So you just go ahead and bite in, and that's when you see that life is sweet. So take life one day at a time, and understand that sometimes, something doesn't look the way that it is. And sometimes it's just taking that leap and understanding and knowing that there's sweetness inside, and that you may just have to avoid that green thing on top.

Enjoy life, know that life is sweet. Do not be afraid to enjoy it. Do not be afraid of judgment. Just do what you love and love the sweetness in life. For the only thing that brings strife between two people is not feeling as if they are sweet enough inside and trying to protect another from them, or protect themselves from another through a reflection of what they believe is a bad heart inside. So when two begin to protect themselves against others, each other, this is the only thing that brings strife in human nature. This is the only thing. For the love that I carry is stronger than one can ever possibly imagine, and I carry this love for every one of my children.

32

(Jude and James)

Muhammed

Joe: Jesus, can we put Muhammad's words into this James and Jude book?

Marisa: "Absolutely not," he said.

Joe: Don't put Muhammed in?

Marisa: Huh-huh.

Joe: Save it for some other time?

Marisa: Uh-huh. He said that will be in three years.

Joe: Okay.

Marisa: He says,

(Jesus) *"You can still continue to talk to him, because he gives you a better perspective of seeing another religion and seeing what's happened, and then you can begin to see your own religion through different eyes as opposed to seeing it from within it. So you can begin to see how things are as you say, "bastardized and convoluted" (throughout religion in general) and then see your own religion and the way this has happened, and you can see that people are just people. People (in the world today) are angry,*

people are upset, people are sad, and this is why the teachings of the higher self or the Holy Spirit or the spirit or whatever you may want to call this, igniting the light within each human being is, oh, so important, because the more lights that are lit, the more lights that are ignited within each human being, the more light is brought to the planet, the more priests are brought to the planet, and this is when the planet will surely survive through the animalistic nature of eat, sleep, kill, mate.

"We bless you, dear ones. We love you, and yes, we thank you, thank you for allowing different energies of different people to come through. We would like to bring other religious leaders to you so that you can get a broader perspective, because there are many, many that, yes, will hear and see and understand my words, but there are also others that we can affect by just hearing from many, many different types of gods."

Marisa: He's talking about all the different gods, like calling in like Zeus and like Poseidon, calling all the different gods, so people can kind of see a different perspective, all the ones from Greece and Rome and –

(Jude and James)

Names in Biblical Times

Marisa: *I think there were two James. Jesus, did you have two brother's named James? He says yes. Can I channel about this, or is my mind going to get stuck in the way? He says,*

(Jesus)   "Oh, my dear brother and sister, what you must understand is that the language in which your books are written in is not the language in which we wrote them in, and the names in which we went by are not the names in which you have within this book. The names that we went by were very different indeed for many of us went by the house we were from, the town we were from, and the name in which we bore with the name of the qualities that we carried. So many times there would be several of the same name in the same family. This was due to the characteristics, but –"

(Jude and James)

Jesus' First Healing

Joe: Jesus, did that happen? Did you keep the roof from falling in, too? James says that you went out and healed an animal who was giving birth, and the roof was falling in, and that was disturbing the animal, whether it was a lamb or it probably --.

Marisa: He says,

(Jesus)   "Yes, I went outside when the hail storm came and it started to cause the structure of the small steeple that we had built for the lamb that was going to give birth." It was like a small tent that was built for the delivering lambs.

Joe: Oh, it was like a palapa?

Marisa: Yeah. They made like a little house for it so that it could lay under there and be safe and give birth.

Joe: From the rain.

Marisa: Yeah, and it wasn't even for the rain. It's like they made it feel safe, or something. It's like they loved the animals just as much as .... well, people would slay the animals to eat them or whatever, but it's like he loved all the animals. He would talk to them. He says:

The Bible Speaks: Conversations with the New Testament Authors

(Jesus) "I would speak to the animals because I saw their spirit inside."

Joe: Like Marisa does.

Marisa: And he felt the spirit inside and he would see the beauty of the father and the mother coming from within the animal in giving birth into a creation that had breath. He says,

(Jesus) "When you see the breath rise and fall, even from a mule, you understand and see that each breath is sacred, each breath brings wisdom and each breath brings knowledge. And although an animal may not have the capacity to speak unto the humans, they surely have the divinity of God within them, for they blink, for they sniff, they smell, for they walk about the earth just as humans walk about the earth, and they think and they sense, just as humans think and sense. But human beings many times believe that they own the earth, when in fact the earth owns the human beings. For when we bring about the beauty of God within each living creature, and we see God in each living creature, it makes us realize that we are just a creation, just like the animal. So I would look upon them, look into their eyes, and I could feel them and sense them. So, yes, my brother James saw when one evening I began to feel a surging in my hands at times. I began to feel a surge within my lower belly at times. I began to feel a surging within my feet, and within my temples. And these were energies that I felt, as if I had to place upon others, or place upon something. So when my hands began to surge, I knew that something needed me to place them upon them. So when the hailstorm came, and the small structure in which we had created for Agah, the name of the lamb, I ran out and I placed my hands upon her, as she was afraid that she would die, she was afraid that she would be smashed upon by the shelter and was afraid to give birth to her child. So I placed my hands upon Agah and brought forth the life in which she was delivering. I did not think that *anybody saw me. But it is apparent now, and of course I know now, that my dear brother saw this and witnessed this. Many a times this happened, especially when in the ministry, in starting the ministry, as my hands would begin to feel the surge, the surge of the heat entering into them, whereby knowing that this needed to be transferred unto somebody else. This was one of the first times I felt this, so much so that I felt and saw light outside of myself."*

Joe: That was the first time he realized his healing powers?

Marisa: It was actually the third time, the third time. *"But it was the first time where"* –. *He's showing it's the first time where he actually went "whoa."*

Joe: *"This is cool."*

Marisa: Yeah.

Joe: Okay. But he wasn't egotistical. He didn't run around going, *"Hey, look what I can do."*

Marisa: No. He says he began to play with the energies. *He began to form energy between his hands, move it along different parts of his body. He's saying that he would feel the different energies and he would soon deliver this account to schools that taught this healing energy. Once his parents knew of it, he was sent to mystery schools, or something like that, where they knew how to work with energy, or something.*

Joe: Really?

Marisa: Yeah.

35

(Jude and James)

James the Just

Joe: Well, in here it mentioned that one James died even before Jesus died. One James died even before Jesus, but in the Bible, after Jesus is executed the apostles tell people that they need to go talk to the brother of Jesus who is 'James the Just' but they don't go into any details. So, who is James the Just? Is that the brother that just – is this something I should be asking now or wait until tomorrow? Who is James the Just?

Marisa: We can ask now. He says....and he's laughing. He says, "There're three 'James the Just' if you really look at it."

Joe: Who was the Bible referring to when they say, "James the Just?"

Marisa: James the Just is a man –

Joe: But they're saying it's your brother. Are they speaking of your brother?

(Jesus) "No.... the word, 'brother' is thrown around a lot...brother, sister, brethren...so in translation, many times apostles or even cousins or close friends were called upon as brothers, sisters, family. It's a term that they used. 'James the Just' is just a character made up in the Bible."

Joe: Oh, great. Ay yay yay. I can't go there...!

(Jesus) *"James the Just is – let me put it this way; as time passes by, as the years went by, people told stories by the fire, people told stories around their – around their homes. Many began to give names, give nicknames – for lack of a better word – to the different personalities of our time. For if you were to call in all of the names that are used to describe people, you would get maybe six to ten different energies coming in. This is why this is a little complicated for us because this channel can see so many dimensions. If she could just see one or two dimensions, then it would not be so confusing, but what she is actually seeing is the morphic fields of made-up characters. She's seeing the spirits, she's seeing the higher selves, she's seeing all the different energies of all the different phases of their life. So what we suggest to you, what we suggest to you is to remind her that when we do this channeling tomorrow to call in the actual human that was my brother, the human being that was my brother that was named James at birth. When you speak unto him you will find that this is the brother that saw me with the lamb.*

(Jesus) *"James is a meaning. James is a meaning, so there would be James of this or James of that or James – James the _."*

Marisa: Like he's showing me James the Happy, James the Angry, James the whatever.

(Jesus) *"So many times we would go by those terms of endearment but this is not like Yeshua Ben Joseph. This is like 'Yeshua the Happy' ben Joseph. It was like Yeshua the Happy ben Joseph... of the Joseph, of this town."*

36

(Jude and James)

Zippers

Joe: Since I know you're going to put zippers over your mouth if I bring up the Bible.... I want to find out if ... and I'm going to be really careful here, but the Bible states, yet we've already been told in these interviews that it's not a virgin birth per se but that was the philosophy of Constantine so they had to basically make up a story. Anyway, we had a lot of problems yesterday trying to figure out James' story and a lot of stuff came through. So we'd like to try to get the real story from the real father or real mother, which would be Joseph and Mary, why we are being told that there were two or maybe three Jameses. I want to know from you, Christ, if it's okay if we converse with Joseph and Mary about this subject.

(Christ)   Absolutely. The truth is already in each and every one of you. The truth is already in there. It's just looking and seeing the truth and allowing the truth to come through as the truth comes through, for the beliefs and the fears and the antagonism that one has for oneself inside of oneself in a human to go against the grain is something that one may fear too much, so we give the truth. Many times you just do not hear the truth. When the channel sees zippers over mouths, sometimes this is because she does not want to hear, and sometimes it is because they do not want to tell

only because they think she or you do not want to hear, but we are an open book. We will give you any information you want. We will answer any question you want, because in universal energy, everything is the same. We are just information particles, and really the information that we give, we have no attachment to. Humans are the ones that provide attachment to certain beliefs, certain things. If one's beliefs are stricken against, one has fear that they will not be able to believe anything that they have ever believed. And then there is also the fear that they will have been wrong their entire life, or they will look stupid, or they will feel ashamed that they believed something that they thought was so clearly something that they feel they should not have believed now that they know the truth.

"So let us just say this. Let us just fill this room, let us just fill this surroundings, including the child, including the animals, with the ability to hear taken information, receive information without attachment, without attachment to what it means, without attachment to "Is this going to go in the book?" without attachment to what people say, without attachment to 'Oh, my goodness, I can't believe that I thought this, and now what are my beliefs?' Let us just fill and surround this room with the ability to listen and hear as if this is fiction and then take from it which you would like, for what we have said and what we said yesterday through one of our own is that it is not about the information. It is not about who did what, who was a virgin, who was not, who slept with who, who was married, who had a child, who did not. It is not about that at all. It is about the human condition. It is about being a human and being conflicted between spirit, body, mind; being conflicted by these things and having a spirit inside that wants to sing, that wants to play, that wants to be in joy, that wants to have fun, and a mind that says, 'You cannot do that, because that is not

responsible. You cannot do that, because that is not fun. You cannot do that because that is fun.' And we say unto you, we say unto you that the earth plane is what you make the earth plane, and yes, we have said this many, many, many times before. We have said this over and over again but we cannot say it enough. We cannot say it enough that you create your own reality. You create your own reality, and you entangle your reality with others. What you choose to take on from their reality is your choice on some level. You may say, 'But my human does not know. My human does not know.' Yes, your human does not know, but your spirit does. Your higher self does. Some level of you does, so all you must do is just ask the questions. Ask the questions. 'Why am I creating this reality? What is this reality being created for?'*

"Joe, when things happen to you and you end up not being able to go and see your fiancé, you have to ask yourself this question: 'Why is big Joe doing this? What am I getting out of this? What am I getting out of it?' This is all you must do, and as soon as you see what you are getting out of it, most cases it changes, because now you've learned your lesson. So understand that – and it is the same for all human beings – we must always ask, why is our higher self choosing this? Because unlike that which this channel believes, yes, lives are programmable and lives are charted out, but they change all the time, and we can change it all the time. We can pull in different guides; we can pull in different higher selves if we want. So we are the makers of our own destiny, and the more the world transfers into and merges into the fifth dimension, the more people will realize that they are the creators of their own destiny. You may ask any question you would like. I give you the stage."

37

(Jude and James)

Joseph, Mary and the Virgin Birth

Marisa: Okay. The higher self of Joseph . . . Yeah, Mary is an angel and so is Joseph. They're both angelic beings. Okay, so Joseph's higher self?

Joe: Yeah. I want to know a little bit about Joseph. I'm going to ask the same kind of questions of Joseph as I did of all the authors.

Marisa: Okay. Here's Christ...

(Christ) "Well, first we must, first we must say, first we must say that yes, thank you. Thank you for calling for the personality, the personality of the man, the personality of the man that reared and brought forth what the stories tell as the man that was God, the man that was God, and we say unto you, we say unto you the stories, we say unto you this because they were stories, there were many stories, there were many stories. There are many, many stories.

"What we would like you to do is to put this into perspective. You receive an email. You read the email, and later on in that day, you want to tell what that email was about to someone that you're talking to. You do not remember all the details, so you just kind of tell what it was about. They then – let us just say it was a joke. So you tell the punch line of the joke. You get to that part, but you don't remember if the person in the boat was wearing red or blue or green or if they were with someone or they weren't with someone, or what they saw or what they felt. You just know the punch line. That person then goes and tells the joke, but they remember more the person was wearing red, this person was wearing green, this person was wearing blue; and because you did not fill in all those details, their mind fills in the details, and then they forget the joke; and then that next person tells it, and on and on and on. And this is all within about 20 minutes of each other. Imagine what happens over 300 years of unintelligent people telling stories to each other about grandiose things that they saw, felt or heard? A simple energy healing that this channel can perform would be considered a miracle in that time. If she was to go into the bible times now, this very moment, she would be considered a high priestess with magical powers. So what one must understand is you must put this into perspective. The consciousness of the planet is going up, and yes, you still get the punch line.

"Someone came down to teach human beings how to live with compassion. That was it. Jesus came to teach people to live from their spirit, not from their mind, and to love themselves and others and to have compassion, and to know and honor the Father or the higher energy within them that is them. This is it, this is all, and this is the basis of many ancient civilization teachings. This is the basis of many teachings. There are many occults, many sects, many religions, quote, unquote, 'religions' that focus primarily on nurturing the spirit, because the spirit is your own individual spirit,

Book V   Ask Jesus

rather than 'I have a Holy Spirit' that every single person has, and we all share the same spirit. Yes, we are all One, but we are also individuals. So there are many religions that support this. What the government did not want at that time and what human beings did not have in their consciousness or awareness was that we are God inside. We are clones of God experiencing life in physical bodies that we have created, that we have programmed and lives that we have designed. So in essence, we are God inside. We are God all around us, so just as we have shared (with you) three days ago that the Holy Spirit is a vehicle, we must just have you continue to imagine this within your mind that you are inside the Holy Spirit and you are eternal, whether you want to imagine yourself as Joe or big Joe or whatever you want to see yourself as, see yourself in a bubble that is the Holy Spirit, and inside you have your spirit's personality. That spirit will continue through, continue through time until you have evolved and ascended. So you must know and you must understand that you are always surrounded by the Holy Spirit, but you are always a Creator God inside.

"Now, we know that you want to ask questions, but we must explain this and reiterate this to you so that you can see and understand how and where all of these quote, 'stories' came from. You must also understand that there are other religions that speak of the virgin birth, the resurrection, the apostles. There are other religions. This is a storyline that has been told throughout all time within the earth plane.

"When entering into the earth plane, it is like entering into a movie that's already been filmed. You look at the movie, you jump into the movie, and you know 'I'm in this movie, so I'm not going to be able to leave Pleasantville,' which is what the movie is. 'I'm not going to leave because it doesn't exist outside of this *movie.' There's nothing in this movie that says that there's a Connecticut and there's a Kansas and there's a California and there's a Washington and there's a Tokyo and there's a Japan and there's a Canada (and Peter says, "And New Zealand,") (lol)). There's nothing here that says that there is something that does not say that is here. It is not within the parameters of the movie. If you look back and you look upon the movie not from within it, you can say, 'Oh, that's Pleasantville. There's all these other towns around it.' But when you're in it, when you are in it, you are in it for the rules that were made around the movie.*

"So you must understand that the earth plane has rules. The earth plane has programs. The earth plane has information databases within its grid. We have spoken of this grid within (your interview with) John in Revelation about this grid where we play unto the earth music, or we play frequencies, we play sounds within the grid that surrounds the planet and this then affects the rules, affects the people, affects the spirits that are inside the people on all dimensions, on all levels.

"So just as John had said in his Revelations, in your book about Revelation, he had said that if we play rock music in the grid of the planet, no one can hear it, but everyone on the planet will soon begin to wear rock t-shirts and bash their heads up and down and dance like they are listening to rock music. But then if we turn the classical music on, the classical music will be turned on into the grid of the planet where all the rules and all the stories are placed, and then everyone will begin to get calm, unless they hate being calm and they will get even angrier. So this is what we spoke of about the white horse, about the peace entering into the earth plane. Peace has been programmed into the grid around the planet.

"Now, back to 2,000 years ago. 2,000 years ago peace came at that time and that peace came in the form of our soul family. For our soul family decided to populate a planet that had not been previously populated necessarily by our soul group but very much by beings that were primitive, the beings were primitive. We had only lived on the planet prior (to these primitive beings) to an ancient civilization that were around prior to the earth destroying itself. The Sumerians brought much information into the grid of the planet with many of the rules that were placed. So when one prays and one says, 'Heavenly Father God, please say unto me what I need to hear and tell me what I need to know,' and they see, 'Oh, there's going to be a virgin birth. There's going to be this, there's going to be that, and an angel of God has come to tell me this,' they could either be tuning into the Pleasantville movie and within the movie that's in the grid, or they could be talking to an angel. So many times when people receive prophecy, many times when people receive information about future events, what they are truly tuning into is a past image, a past story, a past frequency.

"So we say unto you that many foretold the virgin birth. Many foretold this, and this is what the ascended masters entering into and coming into an earth plane had to play by the rules, so this was something that was needing to be accomplished when entering into the earth. For Mary was trained. Mary was trained her entire life in the works of energy and the works of prayer and the works of rights and rituals and Taoism?

Joe: Taoism?

Marisa: Oh, okay.

(Christ continues) "And understood, understood that from where we all come from, we all return. And this was a one-god concept, whereas there were many Jewish people who still secretly believed in the multi-gods of the Greek era, and many that believed in other more esoteric beliefs such as wickenism – paganism. So you must also understand that when you look upon a movie that you need to go into, let us just say that you, Joe, and this channel (Marisa) are going to go live in a movie so you decide, 'I am going to go live in Back to the Future. I'm going to go live in that movie, so I know that I can either be – I can either be Michael J. Fox, I can be the father, I can be the girlfriend, I can be the teacher. I know all of the characters that I can be. Which one do I want to be and which one will be the best for me to accomplish my goal?'

"So I, as Christ, chose seven characters to inhabit at that time as a direct line from here, the eighth dimension. So as I stand here in the eighth dimension as a fully charged, a fully evolved spiritual being I projected my consciousness into seven beings at that time. There have been times where I have been up to 25 beings, so I was not necessarily spreading myself as thin as you thought.

"So I say unto you that I project myself unto Joseph (Jesus' dad). Joseph was a good man. Joseph was honest. Joseph was a little rough around the edges, and I appreciated that. That was something that I enjoyed and the energy of him was something that I enjoyed playing. He was teased when he was young. He was bullied when he was young. He was a bit small. He was a bit short so many people made fun of him. "Mary was raised as a – as a prophetess, as someone who would take over the line of work that her mother, Jesus' grandmother, Anna, was procuring on the planet, for she was working with the earth grid, for she was working with nature, she was working with divine beings, she was working with the elemental kingdom to nurture the earth with

Book V   Ask Jesus

energies to heal people for she made tinctures made of roots. She made many medicines that people would use instead of going to a physician."

Joe: That was Anna or Mary?

(Christ)   Anna. *Anna taught Mary everything that she knew. Mary knew from a very young age that she was special, and this is not to say that she was special because no one else could do what she did, but this was her mission. This was her plan. She was to bring about the Divine Feminine energy, the Holy Spirit incarnate into the earth plane, and she was to give birth to a being that she would train in all of the same rituals, all of the same energy healing, for lack of a better word, all of the same techniques that she learned from her mother. So this was the plan. When you look at someone and you say, 'Oh, wow, they are a professional baseball player. They have such natural abilities.' Yes, but if the parents were not interested in sticking the child in baseball or they did not nurture or take them to practice or say, 'Go out there and practice even though you don't want to,' then the person would not become a professional baseball player because they would not be in an environment that is conducive to them being a success. So in order for Jesus to be the success in which he was he had to be born to a household that held in higher regards the connection between spirit and God through our own means, not having to go through a Rabbi or somebody that can talk to God but other people cannot.*

"*So Mary was trained. Mary was trained, and she was not married off. Mary was trained and she was kept in the highest of regard knowing and seeing and understanding that she would be the one that quote, 'played the part' to birth the quote, 'next messiah.' Mary's cousins, aunts, uncles, grandparents, even those from the court wanted to marry her off when she was twelve. She was not married off for many different reasons, but Anna made sure to keep her in virginity. For understand that when children became women, when they began to menstruate, this is when they became women, and this is when they would be married off. This is when they would be given to another man to take off the father's hands, 'Now you have her. She is yours. You take care of her. She will give you babies.' This is the way that women were looked at, and this was the role that they were okay with.*

"*So she was kept from this for two years until Joseph came along, which was my spirit, my spirit, for understand and know that in order for there to be quote, 'a virgin birth,' in order for there to be something that is procured from nothingness, one must fully understand the spiritual makeup of spiritual DNA, and we will not go into that, but by combining an angelic force and that which is Mary's higher self in spirit with that which is the T body? The T body of Christ, himself –*" (Marisa: he's talking about himself) "*– within a physical body, much can be accomplished between two spiritual beings without ever having physical contact.*

"*So you must understand that everything in the physical becomes physical because it happens in the energy plane first. Your physical body did not exist, but your etheric body did. How did this channel (Marisa) know what her daughter would look like (before and after her pregnancy)? How is that possible? She was not made yet. Is it because she is psychic? No. It is because the etheric body is already created; the life path is already created, the way that she will look is already created, and now that creation, that way that she looks is now in her human field, and due to that, the human field will grow into that. So the human body grows into what the spiritual body is.*

Book V   Ask Jesus

"So when one says, 'is that Joseph's child? Is it Mary's?' it is Joseph's and Mary's, and we say this unto you and this is hard to explain, but yes, it is their child, but no, there was no physical interaction to bring the child into the womb. So you must understand this, though. It was still their etheric bodies, it was still their energy bodies, and when trained in the magical rites of that which is the gnostic and the Isis teachings of that day that came together to bring about these magical rites that many would do that were part of these cults, so to speak, were able to bring their vibration and their energy up so high that they were able to either disappear, walk through walls, walk on water. They were able to leave their body, hang out with other people that had left their body, and this is what they did. They had intercourse in the etheric plane, brought their bodies back into their human fields, and then their human was pregnant.

"So understand this and understand this well, there was a child prior to Jesus. This child died. This child was to be a woman, was to be a girl. This child was to bring the information that needed to be brought in order for them to understand and see and know that Jesus was coming. Yes, they were always foretold of Jesus. They were foretold of Jesus their entire lives, but you must understand that many times because we are blind by the physicality, many times messengers in the form of children that do not survive, messengers in the form of dreams, messengers in the form of angels or deceased loved ones will be sent to the earth plane. If the human beings are not giving the message, many times energies from the other side will get sent down into their field for – to attune the person so that things can take place that need to take place. Does any of this make sense?

Joe: It makes sense. The only question I've got is, did the child that died, was that from the human interaction or was it the etheric realm interaction that created the child that died? And you said it was a girl, and I'm still confused, because we're under the understanding that it was James, and he died or – yes, that it was a boy. So anyway, that's – I think I understand everything you said, but I still have that little question mark.

38

(Jude and James)

Mary and Joseph's Lost First Child

Joe: So anyway, that's my question. You mentioned they had a child. Was it Joseph and Mary in the human physical plane that had intercourse and then they had a child that died, or was it like in the case of Jesus who was conceived in the etheric –

Marisa: "No. That child was in the etheric, in the etheric realm."

Joe: She was too? Was it a girl?

(Christ) "She was as well, but she was not born. She was not born, for she brought the information that she needed to bring. What you must understand, let's look at it like this, let us look at it like this: Let's say that you have a computer, and you want to play a song on it. You want to play the Beach Boys. You want to play Surfin' USA *on your computer. You've heard of it, you know of it, but the computer doesn't know of it. It doesn't understand it. It can't play it. It can't fathom it, because it does not even know what it is. So you cannot just tell the computer, 'Oh, play this song.' It must be programmed into the computer, so you may either find the song on a CD and insert it into the computer and download it onto the computer and then take the CD away and then now it is in the computer even though there is no CD in there, or an SD card or a USB wire to another computer.*

"So what is happening when a child is entering into the womb of a mother is, in essence, information from the upper-dimensional realms is being downloaded into the circuitry or into the energy field of that which is the computer or the person, or the person's spirit. So this girl, Sarah, who then later became the child of Jesus who then also –"

Joe: Wait, wait, wait. Sarah became the child of Jesus?

Marisa: Uh-huh. This is the spirit – oh, it's my guide right here. Hey, Sarah, what's up? Okay. So she's right here.

Joe: We've made a huge leap here. You're saying that Mary and Joseph conceived a child –

Marisa: And it died.

Joe: – in the etheric realm, but it never was born??

Marisa: "It was never born, for she was pregnant for – she was pregnant for 32 days." Thirty-two days?

Joe: So she had a miscarriage.

Marisa: Yeah – no, 3.2 months, sorry, not 32 days.

(Christ) "Three point two months, for she was not showing, she was not married at this point, at this point, because of this: She was betrothed to Joseph. She was betrothed to Joseph, and they were married, for many people, many people never knew of this pregnancy that she had, because she never showed at all; but what happened was the angel or the energy that is – we will call Sarah, because this is how this channel knows it, this energy, and this is how we have spoken of this energy in past channelings with the two of you – is understanding that this higher-self being or this energy downloaded information into Mary and Joseph's field while it was on the earth plane, and then it left. So understand this, understand this: They had to be prepared, the circumstances had to be prepared for that which is the coming of the Christ energy, for she never believed that it would happen. She never believed that it was actually true. She did not believe that anything like that could happen, and when it did, her panic, her fear and her unworthiness of being the carrier of a child that was to change the world caused her to miscarry. So in order to fully encompass and embrace the responsibility that she was being given from birth and being told

from the time she was three years old, she had to experience it first and then have it happen again."

Joe: Are you saying then that her stress and her worry caused a miscarriage of a child that was going to be a girl, but it was going to be a girl messiah?

(Christ) "It was to never be born. The plan was to – "It was just a download. It was like putting Surfin' USA on the computer."

Joe: So it was to prepare her – by losing the first one, it prepared her for the actual birth of Jesus.

(Christ) "And forced her to get married to me, Joseph, Christ."

Joe: Oh, okay.

(Christ) "Forced her to marry me, because –"

Joe: And it wasn't the same spirit in the girl – what was her name going to be? Was there a name?

Marisa: It was Sarah, but her name is A-L-V-O-K-O-V.

Joe: Okay. So let's keep it simple and call it (the fetus) Sarah.

Marisa: Yeah.

Joe: So the spirit of Sarah was still Christ, but that was a lesson. And then so Christ remained as a spirit.

Marisa: That was not Christ. That was a different spirit altogether.

Joe: So it's just a lesson to be learned to prepare her for basically the virgin birth that had been created in the etheric realm.

(Christ) Yes. So it was virgin, but it wasn't virgin. And according to –

Joe: But by human terms, by human, Joseph and Mary didn't have sex, so they didn't have – they didn't conceive of a child here on the earth. They had that union in the etheric realm.

(Christ) In the etheric realm, which is just as real as the physical realm, but yes, we understand. From man's eyes, no physical interaction, but from the etheric eyes, from the spirit's eyes, there was still physical interaction and the two of them remember, they felt it, they know it, and this was something that was planned and brought into union together, but in order to come into union and bring their energies together that the way they were, they had to be married."

Joe: So as an aside, and I don't – I hate to go out on tangents, so this is just a minor tangent, and then we'll jump back again – are etheric unions happening in the world today?

(Christ) "Absolutely."

Joe: There are people on this earth that are considered born by virgin birth?

Marisa: "Oh, no, no, no. The last one happened was 1962, and – yes, actually yes, 1962. There were 7 in 1954. There was 14 in 1960? There were –" they're jumping around the earth.

Joe: Where are all these people who were conceived in the etheric realm? I mean, that's done within my lifetime, it's still within my lifetime. Are some of these people on the earth today?

(Christ) "Many of them are primitive people that need the story of a virgin birth in order to believe and understand the god, so you may find the Bush People out in the middle of nowhere where there is a virgin birth. So you must understand the way to get to a human mind when a human mind is not so intelligent is to do something that is unfathomable to the human mind; and the human mind and the human beings back in that time, it was all about food, shelter, sex, food, shelter, sex, food, shelter, sex. There is not pleasure that came from food. Food was a necessity. Pleasure came from sex. To women it was a duty. This was to bring a child. So to bring a child into the world without having to have that duty, without having to be with a man, this was something that was just beyond all reason, and this is something that will prove that a quote, 'god exists.' Remember, just like we said, the story of the virgin birth is in the Pleasantville movie. It is already programmed. It is in here.

"So the best way for soul families, soul groups to bring acknowledgement to a greater being than themselves is to just play off the same roles, the same plays, the same movie that keeps playing over and over again. So there is a type of people, there is a path of people, there is a tribe of people that just do not believe in anything else other than their people are diminishing. The souls that are living in them are not being nurtured by their higher selves *and by greater dimensional aspects of themselves. So many times, some of the souls will come in and say, 'Okay, well, let's do this. Let's play off this old story that many people have done before, and let's have a virgin birth. Let's have a resurrection. Let's do it.' They plan it, they go, they do it. So it is really, really something that just keeps being done over and over and over, because it's something that continues to wow human beings. Even though human beings will begin to understand as we become more fifth dimensional that the physical body is actually more pliable than the etheric body, because the etheric body is already built. The etheric body is what needed to be downloaded with the information that she (Mary) needed, because the etheric body is already built into a solid structure that will exist and live for this amount of time with exit points and it will live, it will be married to this person, it will do that. It is programmed completely with the entire movie in it. And to make changes sometimes if one is disconnected, something must be sent down to live inside of it to download the information into it. But understand that 3.2 months of pregnancy and then a marriage, and then seven months later, this is when, this is when Jesus was born unto the world."*

Joe: Conceived?

Marisa: *"Born."*

Joe: Well, that wouldn't make sense, because it takes nine months.

Marisa: *"He was early."*

Joe: He was premature?

Marisa: *"Yes."*

Joe: So that's why they went ahead and went to Bethlehem for the census while she was pregnant??!! Because typically a woman who is pregnant would not travel in those days if she was going to be due. So he was born premature then. That explains a lot.

39

(Jude and James)

Miracles and a Premature Birth

Joe: How many months pregnant was Mary when she had Jesus?

Marisa: "Six point four months."

Joe: Wow. That baby should have died. There's like no way that child should have – I mean even today at 6.4 months, it would have to go into intensive care and be isolated for months.

(Christ) "But again, again, this is a miracle. This is a miracle. Miracles needed to be brought unto the earth so those around that did not believe that this was a virgin birth, that did not believe this would say, 'That child should have been thrown to the wolves. That child was weak. That child was born too soon. That child was not born at the right time.' It was also to throw off prophecy, and it was also to throw off those who suspected that Mary would get –"

Marisa: Hold on…. something or someone dark is trying to get into this story.

Joe: I'm just picturing another layer of the Holy Spirit covering our snow globe right now, another smooth layer, another smooth layer just to thicken that snow globe even thicker and thicker. It's clear inside our snow globe but I can see so much darkness outside of our snow globe right now.

Marisa: I know.

Joe: Trying to get in here. Seriously.

Marisa: Uh-huh.

Book V   Ask Jesus

Joe: I mean they want to get in here and just make a mess. Let me ask you: Christ, is this you, Christ? Is what we're learning right now for our highest and best? Is this something that we are going to be passing on to the world, or is this just for our own edification?

(Christ)   "This is for your edification, but it is not to say that it is not true, for what we must explain to you and implement into the minds in which you carry in these bodies is that the more you understand, the better a minister you are, because that is what you are. You are a minister of truth. You always have been, you always will be, for this channel is a minister and a teacher and a healer. You are a minister, a teacher and a healer. So what we must say is you cannot be a minister of truth if you do not know the truth. Do you have to share everything you know? No. Does this channel share everything that she knows? No. You share what applies to the person that you're speaking to at that moment. So we want to bring information unto you so that you can fully understand, and then you can then look back on time on earth and see the synchronicities, see all the other times that us, as the same exact spirits playing over and over, just as you have said the other day, recycled souls, continue to live the same stories over and over and over and over and over on the earth plane within the movie that we call Earth. So the understanding that 6.4 months into pregnancy –"

40

The Bible Speaks: Conversations with the New Testament Authors

(Jude and James)

Compassion

(Rosemary) "Oh, he (the Elder James) was 'Just' – everyone knew that he had a lot of money, and everybody knew that he was like the brother that could help people out if they were in trouble, because Jesus was like the kind and just one and you could tell him all your problems and he would give you advice; and his brother was more of the one that could give you money if you needed help, but he also knew a lot of lawmen, so when Jesus would help the beggars in the town in which they were from, and many were jailed, he was able to get them out."

Joe: James or –

Marisa: Jesus was able to go to James and say, "Hey, could you talk to your friends over there at the government and let these guys out?"

Joe: Oh, okay.

Marisa: So it was kind of like his government connection or something. Is this true? Jesus, is this true? Yeah? He says,

(Jesus) "No not a government connection. It was more along the lines of people were being thrown in jail for stealing bread, and part of my ministry was that no one should get thrown in jail for having to eat."

Joe: So Jesus or James would go pay off the bill – so to speak...

Book V Ask Jesus

Marisa: *Yeah.*

Joe: *...for the money lost, for the bread stolen.*

41

(Jude and James)

The Human Mind is Like a Satellite Dish

Marisa: Samuel's talking about Jude saying that Jude says that when human beings come in and say "don't think these thoughts or you are evil, don't do these things or you are evil, don't do this and don't do that," Samuel is saying that Jude believes that to be the dark side coming in.

(Jesus) *In a sense between light and dark the egoic mind, the judgmental mind, the gluttonous mind, if we are speaking of light and dark, that would be darker than the light, so it depends on how you look at things.*

Human beings are quite interesting. The natural fetters that they have and come upon are quite amusing to us at times. But we are also souls, we are also consciousness. We have just far exceeded the conscious level that human beings on earth are at, at this time. But it is quite endearing to us to come and to help the future souls of our planet, for we view this almost as a training ground for the souls that will evolve and enter into our worlds, into our dimensions. For the souls have to start out somewhere. But to watch all of the planets where souls begin and carry a newer vibration than the older souls, it is quite interesting to us to study and watch as man claims to be god.

Man plays the god role. Man finds a way to make another man not feel worthy of god. And to this we find quite interesting and stand back and watch as man gives his power away. But we encourage, and this we do unto this channel, to take back your power, take back the love, take back the god inside, understand and know that ye are all gods. And once one understands this, the soul is ignited, that as you say the Holy Spirit is ignited, and within that and that understanding, man can be free, you can be free. For, every thought that goes through your mind is not just your own thoughts. Thoughts that go through your mind are thoughts of others who are passing you by, other's energy who is in your energy field (seeping into your Show Globe) and others who are thinking about you. If they are thinking about you, their thought patterns go into your field. For, the mind that is in the human being does not always think the thoughts of its own. For, the mind, the mind is like a radar dish, satellite dish. It picks up other thoughts of other people. And if the mind is constantly thinking "If I think that I will be bad, even if I do not do it," this is what harms human beings and makes them feel poorly upon themselves. So, in reviewing and listening to your conversation with the man Jude, not the higher self of Jude but the man Jude, this is the summary in which we are giving.

42

The Bible Speaks: Conversations with the New Testament Authors

(Jude and James)

Introducing Judas

Joe: Okay. Let me ask Jesus then. Jesus, when you chose Judas to be one of your apostles, did you know then, right then and there, that he was going to be the one that would betray you?

(Jesus) No.

Joe: Did you know you were going to be betrayed at some point? You had to, because the Old Testament.

(Jesus) Twenty-three days before.

Joe: Only days before?

(Jesus) Twenty-three days prior. But I knew that my life would have to come to an end because ... I was told by the greater spirits.

(Abraham) Judas must be interviewed, for there is an integral story, a part, within history that involves him.

Joe: Yeah, he betrayed Jesus.

(Abraham) For, there are many people that were used as examples in the Bible so as to threaten/teach people not to do the same.

Joe: I'm not sure what that means.

Book V   Ask Jesus

(Jesus)   So, when the Bible was written, there were stories of those who betrayed and consequences that came from or a feeling of guilt that was displayed through the writings, so that others would not follow in that type of behavior, and others would follow the behavior of those that they read about that were saint-like, but interviewing him (Judas) will be a good way to get all sides of the story. So when we bring in these apostles or authors, you may just interview the authors or you may call in those who really wrote it, the scribes, or you may call in any of the apostles.

Marisa: I was just channeling Jesus and we're talking to Judas right now about why he turned Jesus in. So Jesus says,

(Jesus)   "If you can look at each one of these stories and you can look at each one of these tales, you can truly see at the emotional level what all of these lessons were for. If you look at Judas, you look that he was discovered, something was discovered that he had hidden deep inside. He was a prideful man in the sense that he always wanted to do God's work. He always wanted to grow up and be a part of something great, and then he succumbed to human instincts. He succumbed to instincts of man, went outside of the home of the one that he was betrothed to and unto that brought about what you would call bastard children.

But we must say unto you that each one of the stories that we tell, each one of the stories that we tell within the Book of Life, as James called it earlier, the Book of Life are stories that can be looked at at an emotional level. Everyone looks at this as more of on the physical level where he turned him in, he's a bad person, he got Jesus killed; but what many don't realize and see is that yes, yes, just as we have just mentioned in this transcription that you are reading, Joe, is that there was a plan. There was a plan, and this was to be enacted.

The Bible Speaks: Conversations with the New Testament Authors

43

(Jude and James)

Book V   Ask Jesus

Everyone has a Plan

(Jesus)   Just as you have a plan, just as your daughter has a plan, even Poochie has a plan for everyone and every mammal has a plan. So to feel sorry for me, to feel bad for me, to say, 'Oh, poor Jesus. He died on the cross,' this is something that is unnecessary. It's to look at these lessons and to look at the teachings in which I brought. The teachings that I brought were compassion for Man. There was no compassion at this time when I chose to incarnate. There was no compassion. It was survival of the fittest. It was – it was every man for himself, and truly men, yes, they would take care of the women, because the women were pregnant and they were having children, but many of the women were completely oppressed in the Jewish faith.

44

The Bible Speaks: Conversations with the New Testament Authors

(Jude and James)

Women and Men are equal in God's Eyes

(Jesus) *In the religion in which I was raised in by my grandmother, in the belief system in which I was raised in, women were powerful, women were matriarchs, women deserved respect. So what we brought in was an understanding that women and men alike are just as important in God's eyes and can bring about a change on the planet. When I taught this alongside Mary and my mother we brought about something that scared the Jews, that scared the government, that scared the men, because we said that women are just as powerful, women bring life, bring birth, bring us into existence, but not only that, they have the energy and the love of the Holy Spirit naturally within them. Men have to dig for it. Women can naturally encompass this and pull this from within."*

Marisa: *He's saying that's like the intuition. He says,*

(Jesus) *"So if you start to look at this, just take yourself outside of these teachings, Joe. Take yourself outside of these teachings and just look at this, look at this not as – not as a Bible, not as a text written by God, not as anything that is sacred, and just look at the stories and how they've been placed in here, and look at them metaphorically and look at the emotions and the feelings that come behind each one of them. You will see that each one of the apostles that are mentioned all carry a characteristic of the ego that the human mind is made up of. Each of the stories in the Bible always have something to do with an ego characteristic squashing out – for lack of a better word – the spirit inside or the Christ within. So what we are bringing forward today, what we are*

Book V   Ask Jesus

bringing forward today is an understanding of, yes, Jude, James, my brother, yes, I had two brothers named James, what you must understand is that even though I died fairly young, my mother lived to 102 years old."

Joe: Wow. Wow.

Marisa: What?

Joe: Wow.

45

The Bible Speaks: Conversations with the New Testament Authors

(Jude and James)

Mary lived to 102 and Joseph 87

(Jesus) "My mother lived to 102 years old. This was unheard of. This was something that no one could ever possibly imagine. In fact, she took on a different name after a while because she wanted her identity hidden."

Marisa: What? Okay, hold on. Back up. Am I – is this Jesus? He says,

(Jesus) "It's me. It's me."

Marisa: Okay. So Mother Mary lived to 102? What about Joseph?

(Jesus) "87."

Joe: That's like an ungodly amount of time to live back then.

Marisa: Why did they live so long?

(Jesus) "They knew how to preserve, they knew how to heal the human body, and they knew how to bring etheric matter into form. My mother knew how to make tinctures. She knew how to make medicine. She knew how to heal by touch, and this is where I learned this when I was young. Many of my brothers and sisters carried the natural abilities that my mother carried, and in her divine plan she chose to stay on the earth and have children and pass along the teachings that she so loved and desired and the teachings that I taught.

Book V   Ask Jesus

The teachings that I taught are not Christian teachings. They are the teachings that my mother and my grandmother passed down to me and my brothers and sisters. They are the teachings that we learned from our one true God, that we are spirit in human bodies, and we need to appreciate and love our human bodies, and we need to nurture our human bodies and live happy lives and not be afraid of a wrathful, vengeful god. We on a regular basis in our home heard from angels, because my mom and my grandmother spoke to them. They spoke tongues and they brought through valid sacred texts and information that we all learned about."

46

(Jude and James)

Spiritual Amnesia and Your Plan

Marisa: *And Jesus is saying this to you Papa ...*

(Jesus)   *"Just as your father played the part he needed to play, everybody plays the part they need to play to add to the human consciousness and awareness that God is God. And god is within each of us.*

So we each had a role, but we did not necessarily know what that role was when we were in human form, because we did not remember what that role was (after birth). But, prior to entering into the matrix of earth we knew what those roles would be. So yes, at a soul level we all knew, we knew the plan, we knew the play, we knew the idea of what would be happening, we all planned it, we all went in knowingly what would happen but once in, just as both of you know ...

Joe: *... we don't remember ...*

(Jesus)   *... we don't remember. But that aspect that does remember, that piece of us that resides within us that remembers all is the reason why we did what we did so that each and every human being living at this time could know that you are god. You carry god within you and you create your life the way that you would want god to create it; the way that you would love it, the way that you would want it to be. So when you ask upon the Father, when you ask upon that god-source within you, you know that you are the one that created this life, you are the one that created all this, and to look onto it and even say 'oh, my angels or my guides will make this happen,' you must say and must know, and you must*

know at the very deepest, deepest, deepest part of your being, that you are the one that instructed these guides to help you to do this.

So you must know and understand and see the power that you carry within, the power that you carry within you and around you. So know that each and every day that you breathe a breath, know that each and every day that you breathe life into that beautiful, divine body in which you live in at this time, know that we are all one, yes, and we say this a lot, and nobody truly understands what this means, but if you were to truly, truly embody that which is the one, which is God, we would all be the same, we would all be the same person, we would know all of the same things. And, you do know all these things.

So know, each of the two of you, understand that as you continue to have these conversations with us, as you continue to have these conversations, you will see and you will understand that the awareness that is brought about you is growing, the awareness that is brought within you is growing. And your life will change. Your life is changing. And you will see that much more light is brought within you to carry throughout unto others. For others may feel disruptions in their life because of your light. For many of the things that they do not deal with on a day-to-day basis, you come into their life and these will be uplifted in their life, and they will begin to deal with these things, and go through things that they have not gone through at a much faster rate than they have. For, the two of you are healers and you bring this light into each other's and those around your lives. So be patient, be kind and understand and know that you are bringers of light, you are ministers of truth, and we are proud. We are proud of the two of you. We bless you and bid you a good night."

Joe: Amen. Thank you, Jesus.

The Bible Speaks: Conversations with the New Testament Authors

47

(Peter and John)

These are the Shoes in Which I Walked

Book V   Ask Jesus

Joe: The Christian community, the Churches I go to, are going to rip me for doing these books. They think that my being able to hear Jesus means I'm either evil or crazy. Well, I don't hear him but you do. At least I get to ask questions that he answers.

Marisa: Here, here's Jesus....

(Jesus) We come together today to embark on this mission to understand that in walking this path that it is not an easy path. In walking this path, there will be ridicule. There will be defamation of character, and there will be those who will remarkably make you feel that way about yourselves. This is what one must understand and already one is feeling judged. We do not want anyone to feel judged. We do not want anyone to feel as if information is being given to them so that they have to make a moral decision on whether to share it or not. What we bring in today, what we bring in today is information that will help uplift, uplift the planet, help uplift the world. And by the ego, the ego sometimes gets a hold of this and feels as if we're judging so please do not feel as if you're being judged for we would not be bringing in this information, we would not be here. We would not be allowing you to hear our words. We would not be channeling through this particular channel unless these words wanted to be heard.

Please know that these are the shoes in which I walked. This is the life in which many walked, but please do not see yourself as martyrs or victims. Do not see yourself as, 'I have to suffer in order to get the Words out' for you may feel like this from some. We speak to the channel (Marisa) in this case mostly and understanding that the words, the words that we speak through you are not to be judged by you or others. Others will judge this, but they are not judging you. They are judging our words, not yours. So please know, please know that as you ask these questions, as you move forward in this, in staying in integrity, in staying in honesty (we) will bring through the answers in which we feel, we feel will be good for humankind at this time. For you will, you will learn much. You'll learn much and you will share this information. We'll not bring through anything that will damage or hurt anyone in any way for this is something in which we are not here to do. So please know, please know that if there's any negativity, negativity being sought after, this is not something that we'll answer. This is something that I will facilitate in shutting down. So please know, please know that we are bringing this in as a ministry. We are bringing this in as a ministry and you are disciples, disciples of Christ, disciples of me in understanding and taking complicated knowledge, complicated knowledge that will become simplistic, simplistic for others to understand.

Joe: I'm still going to be judged by my peers but thanks for the encouragement.

(Jesus) Please know to not feel judged – and, you are very welcome. Please know not to feel judged for you are not being judged. You are my brother. You are my sister. You are my family. We are all family and as soon as humankind can understand not to worship me, not to worship me, to understand that I am one of you just like you are each one of each other then the worship will go away.

48

Book V   Ask Jesus

(Peter and John)

"Jesus be with me"

(Jesus)   Envisioning the earth, envisioning the earth as a heaven, as one of the layers of heaven is something in which you need to do, understanding that this is the third level of heaven so to speak, and understand that there are many things that are trying to bring heaven down, down below earth.

So understand that we are warriors, we are fighters, and we are here to bring this light, bring this light into the earth plane, into the consciousness, into the grid that surrounds this earth, not only on the physical plane, but in the minds and the hearts and the souls of all of those who reside on the earth plane and in the astral plane on the other side, the other side, quote, unquote, of the earth plane.

Please know that this is much bigger than you think it is. This is very much bigger than you think it is for understanding that when you bring our energy in just the pure and simple fact that when somebody prays and asks for I, Jesus, to enter into their life, I am infusing their aura or their grid with the light of Christ, with the light of the Father, and I am infusing this.

Some may hold this for a very long time. Some may only be able to hold this vibration for a minute or two so that they may have an epiphany, so that they may connect with their higher selves so that they may connect with their guides or angels to give them a message. Sometimes, sometimes the connection is directly to me and this is the information in which I send down.

So when the Christians pray, "Jesus, be with me," I am with them. I am with them and I can be with everybody at the same time for I have been Christed and many of the Christed souls can be in many places in many times in all time.

49

Book V   Ask Jesus

(Peter and John)

Curiosity

(Jesus)   Your curiosity, your curiosity far outreaches beyond the logic, the logic that is carried within each one of your minds, so the curiosity is really what drives, really what drives you and this is good. We are proud of you. We are proud of both of you. We are proud to say that each of you are doing a very good job in the spiritual development in which you are doing.

So know that this book, this book will be something that is written, that is written and read by others that are curious, curious. So the undertone of this book will be curiosity. And this is a humble, high-vibrational, child-like curiosity and this is good.

50

The Bible Speaks: Conversations with the New Testament Authors

(Peter and John)

Religion

Joe: When Jesus is referring to religion, he is not talking about the Church of Christ only. What he's talking about, I'm assuming is --.

(Jesus): What I speak of, what I speak of indeed, is anything created by man to explain God's work. Anything created by man that is for profit that is to explain God's word. So there are many religions, there are many groups of people whom come together that you may call cults. I will call these religions as well. For, every religion is a religion in this sense. It is not just Christianity. It is not just the Church of Christ. It is not Judaism. It is not Muslims. It is not Buddhists or Hindus, Sikhs, Taos.....it is all of them. For, all of them are man-made in explaining some sort of deity, explaining some sort of godhead, explaining some sort of entity or being that will save these human beings from the atrocity of the human experience.

And what I mean by bringing healing to this religion is bringing an understanding and knowing that man did create the Bible. Man did create all of these books, all of these books where people will come in and say 'these tablets were written 6,000 years ago so they must be correct'. So is the Bible. People must understand that just because something is old, it does not necessarily make it true. So there was still man-made intervention done for many things even ancient Egyptian texts, even ancient *stone tablets. Many people will say, "Well this must be true." Well I say, man still wrote them. God did not write these things. So I bring in a healing aspect to religion, whereby people can still have their beliefs, still believe in their deities, still believe in their Christ, still believe in all of these things, but also to understand that that is not all there is, and that religion is not necessary to have a true connection with the god within, or as you two call it and we call it, the Holy Spirit.*

For the church controls many of the minds of the human beings and this is okay. This is okay in that the human beings that understand that rules are needed in order to behave themselves, this is okay. But the world is changing and as we have told you in past sessions, the world is changing and people are becoming aware that there is just a little bit more than – there is a little bit more to creation than what the Bible has said, than what the Bible has said indeed.

So, understanding that you can go directly to God, understanding that each human being can go directly to God, directly to Christ, directly to the Masters, directly to the teachers, directly to anybody, so to speak, they will understand that you do not need to go to a minister. You do not need to go to a spiritual teacher. You do not need to go to a medium. You do not need to go to a healer. This is something that is God-given, God-given.

(Jesus continues): If you want to call it the Holy Spirit or you want to call it the internal soul, if you want to call it a piece of source, call it whatever you may, but this piece inside of each human – each human being is a direct connection with me and with the Father and with any other master that is within creation, within the tree of creation in which God has created.

51

(Peter and John)

Parable of the Radio Station

(Jesus)   *You must look at us as radio stations, radio stations where it does not matter how many radios are tuned into our station. It does not affect the way that we speak. It does not affect our strength. It does not affect the way that we preach or minister. We are simply here speaking, and anyone who chooses to tune into our radio station, so to speak, is able to do that. The only difference between a radio station and us is we are able to infuse you with our energy.*

52

(Peter and John)

Parable on the Light Bulb

(Jesus)   *If you look at each person as energy, you look at each person as a light bulb. You understand that one may be going dim and this is when the light bulb begins to go out for it has not had a recharge in a long time. So asking, asking I, Jesus, or the Father or the angels or the guides or the higher self to come in and recharge the light bulb will help that light bulb, that human being, see much more clearly what they need in their life.*

For we do not come in and say, "You must go left. You must go right." When we come in and we brighten the light bulb, we brighten it so that the human being may with their free will make that decision and they may be able to – and they will be able to see their higher self maybe with their – not with their eyes, but they'll be able to hear or feel or sense or get a gut feeling on what they need to do next. And this is the higher self that is directing and the higher self that knows the plan, the higher self that understands what needs to happen when the human being is on the earth plane.

53

(Peter and John)

The Higher Self / The Soul of Jesus

(Jesus) The higher self is the human being, so to speak, and this is the piece of me that communicates with the piece of you for our higher selves to communicate. <u>For I am the higher self.</u> I am the higher self of the incarnated spirits that were Jesus and other Masters in that time, for I evolved just like you. I evolved just like you and what you speak of right now is the higher self, the higher self.

Joe: Does that mean you're Christ?

(Jesus) In speaking with the Christ Consciousness, in speaking with the Christ Consciousness, you are not able to speak to one person, one person, for the Christ Consciousness is an aspect of God. The Christ Consciousness is an idea of God. Christ Consciousness is – if you want to say good and bad (the Christ Consciousness) is the good in the universe. So speaking with the Christ Consciousness is not speaking with an individual. It is speaking with everybody. So by communicating with me, with the soul, the soul that was created by the Christ Consciousness just as you were created by the Christ Consciousness, you are speaking with that which understands and knows the life of Jesus Christ.

54

(Peter and John)

Worshiping

(Jesus) For when one worships, when one worships, they are placing themselves in a lower vibration. They are placing themselves down on their knees, and this is okay to show respect. This is okay to show respect for this is something that was done in the old times, in the old times to show this respect, to take oneself below the person in which they are bowing to.

Joe: People are lowering their vibrations by praying or worshiping?

(Jesus) That came out a little skewed with the Channel. What we are trying to say is when people worship, their vibration does become raised when they believe that they are worshiping something that they love. Not in placing themselves down below that. Like a child would look up at their parent and say "that is my parent and I admire him, he is amazing and that is my parent and I am proud." That would raise the child's vibration because it raises up their worth because they are the child of that great parent. So in essence it raises one's vibration when they are to pray and to heed the words of whom they are worshiping.

But when one, just as we said in this case, begs through worshiping, pleads, cries for forgiveness, this is a lowering of one's vibration. So when we speak of this, we speak that we can go directly to God. And when I say that people need to not worship, I do not mean they do not <u>need</u> to worship. For many enjoy the worshipping aspect of religion. Many enjoy the worshipping aspect of God in that they are proud of God and want to thank God, and want to praise the words in which God says. But too many, too many, in fact 82% of the world's population that worships, worships as a lowly servant of God; a lowly servant that does not deserve God's eyes, even for just one moment. For they cover themselves and they say "I am dirt, God, I am spit, I am dirt on someone's shoe and I do not deserve your love, I do not deserve your respect and I come to you and I plea and I cry and I beg for your love and I beg for your respect. This is what I speak of when the words that we hear in people's minds and the words that we hear in people's prayers come to us in this fashion for this is the lowering of the vibration that we speak of.

But please know, please know there are too many people on this earth plane that feel that they need to worship or plea or beg or beg for forgiveness, and this is not something in which they need to do for when somebody begs it lowers their vibration down to unworthiness; and when one feels unworthy, one becomes defensive, one becomes angry, one becomes revolting, and they take this out on other human beings and they blame other human beings for being the things that they are. For everybody's a projection of themselves, everybody is a mirror, everybody only sees their own attributes unless they're trained to not see this, until they are trained to see others for what others are.

But when we say people sing, they praise and they worship, this is raising one's vibration in pride that they have a deity or a god or someone that they so look up to, that they so look up to. But in looking up to, in looking up to this just as we have said, everybody is a projection, as you can ask 10 people what their favorite qualities of their quote/unquote "god" is, and you will find that the qualities that they share are qualities that they have. So one may say, "I love my god because he is humble and he is kind," and you will find that the person that says this is humble and kind. If you find that somebody says that he is vengeful and wrathful, you will find that that person also carries those qualities.

So just as we have said, not only do people project their own behaviors and their own thoughts and their own opinions onto others, and accuse others of what they are thinking and what they are actually doing, they also see themselves in God. For we are all a reflection of God and God is a reflection of us for we are all created in his image, in his image indeed. And when we say we are all created in his image, we do not mean man was created in God's image. We say the <u>souls</u> are created in God's image. The souls just incarnate into what we call the humanoids, the beings. But God is not a man. God is not a man at all.

So please know that when we come in, we come in, we are taking the "worship" out of what people must do when they speak with me. They must speak with me as a friend. Yes, we know that they respect me. For everybody should respect each other. It is much easier to respect somebody that you've never known, that you've never talked to, that you've been told stories about that is amazing in the stories. It is much easier to respect that but it is also much easier to feel unworthy and to feel judged, and this is what we would like to remove. This is what we would like to remove indeed.

55

(Peter and John)

The Spirit of the Bible

(Jesus)   There are some things left unspoken that are much, much better than being spoken, for a tainted view of that which was put into the Bible, God's words, so to speak, which I like to call man's word of what God said, but understanding that a tainted view of this can ruin some people, for if one says, "Oh, I believe in the Bible," and they still feel unworthy, but they still believe in it, they believe in the Bible, but they don't truly connect to Jesus, what they are doing is they're connecting with the higher vibration of the Bible.

The Bible actually has a spirit, so to speak. Everything has a spirit if you want to speak of a spirit as energy. So look at it as every single thing that exists on this planet has a snow globe. And every single snow globe has a different vibration and different voltage of light bulb. So the Bible carries its own snow globe and this is a much higher vibration than any man can truly tap into, that any many can truly, truly accomplish in a lifetime, or a vibration that man can accomplish. So even when people may not believe in – that they are not worthy of Jesus or worthy of God or worthy of the angels, still believing in the Bible carries them through.

Joe: Who was just speaking to you? The Christ Consciousness?

Marisa: *Jesus's higher self.*

56

(Peter and John, Heaven Speaks and The Snow Globe)

The Snow Globe

Marisa: Hold on, here's Yeshua (Jesus) to explain:

(Jesus):   What we would like to explain to you is the Light coming from each and every Higher Self down into the physical body of that being is strong. Inside that physical being there is the Holy Spirit, the Soul. Inside that physical body, that Soul has experiences that have been carried throughout from past lives. The Holy Spirit is still strong within that soul…within that human body.

By turning over the will, the life, to God, as you say, one is opening oneself up and allowing God to shine down into and through the crown chakra *(*top of your head where your soft spot was when you were a baby*)* of the physical body, down through the energy centers, and connect with the Holy Spirit within. See this field as a big globe, a big "Snow Globe".

The light shining from above is God, is Christ, and shining down into the middle of this snow globe is the statue in the middle, *and that is you, the human being, and that statue inside carries the Holy Spirit. When that statue then acknowledges that Light of Christ that shines down, that guides them, that leads them each and every day, it opens them up to connect with the Holy Spirit. The Holy Spirit is ignited by the Light that shines directly down into that statue and lights the fire within. This is that burning desire that humans feel to do good. This is that burning feeling; this is that tear they drop when they have done good and they know they are good. When they experience emotions, when they experience human emotions, just as we have mentioned in the past; human emotions cause fog inside that snow globe.*

Every time that statue experiences something negative or something they "believe" is bad, fog will be created. When one does so many things that they believe are bad but that God may not see as bad, but the earth sees as bad, that fog thickens and thickens and thickens and thickens. The fog thickens so the light coming from above isn't as strong any more. The Light becomes scattered due to this fog. The Holy Spirit still burns within which is the desire to connect with God to lead that physical being back to the arms of the loving creator. That Holy Spirit still burns with that desire, so when this human has the fog of human emotions like guilt, anger, and despair filling up their field, their snow globe, this is when depression sets in and this is when real human instinct will kick in.

Humans without souls are not necessarily good, so to speak, as civilization today would call it. They are mammals. Humans are creatures of instinct, just like animals. They eat, they sleep, they kill, they protect themselves, and they mate. This is what humans do. So in order to fully understand and feel the Holy Spirit within, one needs to ask if their snow globe will be purified by the Light of Christ and have these emotions, the sadness, the despair, removed. As this statue sitting in the middle of the snow globe asks for help, this fog dissipates, is taken away and is enveloped with the Light of Christ. Therefore, the Holy Spirit is reignited back within that statue. So the Light never goes out (extinguished). What happens is interference is caused by the fogging of guilt. Humans feel guilt. Guilt is the biggest killer among human beings. One may begin completely connected with the Light and the Holy Spirit. They may not be religious, but they are a child, they are innocent. The Light of Christ is flowing through them igniting their Holy Spirit and this is their childhood. As they begin to be hurt and told not to do that, or "you're not supposed to do this," guilt begins to build. This guilt begins to block the connection between God and the Holy Spirit within each soul.

As this child grows, this child learns rules, and this child might do things that are wrong. This may be a very dogmatic, religion-ruled household that this child is born into, and soon they will build up massive amounts of guilt, therefore blocking them from their creator. Guilt causes one to look outward at another's guilty nature. It is human-nature; it is the ego's nature, to not look at oneself for what one has done when one feels guilt. One will not look at the things they have done, they will look at what others have done so that the ego feels better. Does this take away the fog? No, it deepens it because inside, the Holy Spirit, the Holy Spirit inside them, knows they are pointing fingers at others for things that they have done.

So this is the human condition that runs rampant throughout earth. This is the human condition of the ego, of the emotions. The more people that understand, the more souls that understand that each and every human being on this planet is their brother; that they are all one, the faster they will clear the fog from their arena, their snow globe, their life and each and every human being will become more and more connected not only to themselves above, their Christ self, the Holy Spirit, their Higher Self, but they will also understand that they are all connected as one. They will realize that up above they are all one.

We bring to you this information in hopes that the words will be spread throughout your society to help these human beings to clear their fog. Healers like your daughter, Marisa, help those people to clear the fog in their snow globes, so to speak. You, Joe, help people to clear that fog in the words that you preach. You are a minister. This is the archetype that you carry. You preach and you carry the words of Christ and through your doing this, by honoring us, we are proud.

We thank you for this and tell you now that you will help many to clear the fog from their Snow Globe that they call their life, their energy or as your daughter and all of her coworkers in the healing field would call and the metaphysical world would call, the aura. Clearing these hardships, clearing these damages to the human aura will help society completely. And sometimes the knowledge and knowing that the religion that someone was brought up in, the household they were brought up in, and realizing and knowing that the words you speak that explain that, then maybe they weren't so bad, maybe these rules were man-made and maybe, just maybe they'll believe that God loves them no matter what. Maybe their Higher Self planned it this way? Maybe it's not all their fault, maybe it's their human nature, it's their ego; it's their emotions. This is not to blame bad behavior on the ego or emotions, but for one to completely understand that in turning their life and their will over to their Higher Self or God, or the Christ within, aka the Holy Spirit, one can begin to see their life as not being a life that is happening "to" them but a life that is in the palms of their hands. They may create the life that they desire and come to realize that life is not just happening to them.

Book V   Ask Jesus

As people begin to understand this information and they begin to see and know that there is a Light within them, regardless of whom or what they believe in, as long as they can believe that there is something greater than themselves then the Light above, guiding and leading them, whether it be Christ, their Higher Self, their Soul, or Angels or Guides, does not matter as long as they believe that there is a Light greater than them, above them, guiding them and they can turn their will in life over to that higher being and the Holy Spirit will be ignited within them. This does not just have to be done only within the Christian faith. This can be done in any way a human mind and ego wishes. The key here is turning the ego and the will of the emotions over to the Light.

Joe: The Snow Globe.... what a good lesson.

Marisa: He says the Snow Globe will change the world.

57

(Peter and John)

Parable of the Hologram

Joe: I asked him to be with me tonight in church and to be with the pastor. Was he there tonight at church?

Marisa: He says absolutely. He says he's everywhere and nowhere all at once.

(Jesus) There is no place that you will find me and there is no place that you will not find me. If you see here ....

Parable of the Hologram

(Jesus) .... that what you are speaking with is a holographic image of who I am then you may look at it this way: this holographic image is just as real as I am. You may look at it like this: when one speaks in an interview on the television and they say words that are great or words that are good, this makes people happy. Therefore, the essence of that person energetically, the person speaking on the television, their energy is in fact in each one of the rooms that the people who are viewing the television have. So please try to see it that way. When a Christian calls in, or anyone calls in, Christ, Jesus, me, they are simply turning the TV on so they may feel and hear the words in which I am speaking, and in doing this subconsciously they are becoming protected, raising their vibration (and) therefore negativity cannot get

through and the negative spirit realm cannot get through. For the spirit realm is very tricky and many a times it's warred against. There are many people that misuse this. But understanding that we are spirits living here, understanding that we are spirits living here is something that is much greater than many people understand or believe, and this is why we come with ministries to teach people that they can do just as much or more than I ever displayed 2,000 years ago.

58

(Peter and John)

Humor

Marisa: Rosemary made it sound like you were humorous and would joke and kid around. Is that true because there is zero humor about you in the New Testament. The Bible makes it sound like everything about your life was so dark and serious.

(Jesus) No I was not as exuberant as she says that I was. But there were many who felt so much joy when around the group of apostles, around the ministry, that they became almost fanatical. They became very happy. So any words that were spoken they would become happy and excited. I used light hearted laughs to help to cheer up the group. For the group would get down and low very often, feeling like they were awkward...like they did not fit in. For their passion in Christ, their passion for the Truth, superseded that of the ego but when they were tired and when they were down, the ego would emerge, and they would begin to discipline themselves, so to speak, in their head, so I would cheer them up, tell stories, make them laugh. So these are things that all of us did, though, it was not just me. Everybody told stories around the campfire. Everyone told stories as we walked. There was nothing else to do but to talk when you're walking miles upon miles upon miles to the next destination. So many stories were told and some

were recorded and some were not. Again, just as we have said, what is recorded in words is not everything that was said. And many of the words that were recorded and stories that were recorded were removed from existence.

59

(Peter and John)

More on Humor

Joe: In about two weeks there's a movie coming out called <u>Son of God</u>. It's about your life, Jesus. Have you seen it? Were you a part of the makers of that movie? Has he seen it? And if he has, if you have, do you think they adequately portrayed your life?

(Jesus) I of course know of, as you say, this movie, but many of the movies that have become popular, that have been viewed by those that believe in Christ, and written by those, I have been an inspiration. Jesus has been an inspiration. Jesus the man has been ---

Marisa: Hold on, he's switching back and forth between his higher self and him. The higher self (Christ) is saying:

(Christ) Jesus has been the inspiration for many, many a poem, many a book, many a movie, and each person that writes these hears him differently, just as if another channel was to be sitting next to this channel, they would be hearing different things. So know that it goes through the mind the way that the mind knows how to generate the thoughts. They will get something similar but it

will not be exactly the same. So in answer to the question, no, I have not seen it but it was inspired by me. [Now he just jumped back over to Jesus.]

Joe: The writers of the movie were Roma Downey, who played the angel on Touched by an Angel, that television show, and her husband Mark Burnett. A short piece of it was shown at the church tonight, and then a guy came on, one of the singers from the band, and said that he was fortunate to see a pre-screening of the movie and he said there wasn't a dry eye in the theater. So once again this movie is going to continue to portray Jesus in a---well, my feeling is they're going to continue to portray Jesus as a vulnerable person who people take advantage of and then everybody feels bad for Jesus. That's why I wanted to bring up (the subject) about the humor because it's not in the Bible. Nothing's in there that says that Jesus wanted to keep people happy. Everything is so sad.

(Jesus)   In order to get people to believe and get people to feel guilty enough to behave, quote/unquote "God," they must feel as if they are ....

Marisa: He's going back and forth. Here, I just want to talk to either Jesus or talk to.... okay, the higher self. That's a lot easier. Can my higher self or Eden help translate? Somebody please?

Joe: Are they speaking in a language you don't understand?

Marisa: Yeah, but it's translating through my head as English. What was the question? Oh, the humor....

(Christ)   So understanding that human behavior is that of the ego, human behavior is that of what we would call the deadly sense, these are all the characteristics that the human being *carries. But understand that the spirit is free, the spirit is fun, the spirit is joyful and blissful and full of glee. As human beings begin to live more in spirit, less in the physical, you will see that things are not that serious over here. We kid around, we joke, we have fun, for just because we have incarnated into the physical body does not mean that we need to be so serious. This is not going to say that Jesus was not a serious person in the sermons, in the message in which he was transferring to the human beings at that time. But if a human being was to be so serious all the time, people would grow bored. For human beings are habitual creatures but also animalistic creatures that need to be entertained. For you go to a church that is very serious and you are not encouraged to go back because you just sat for two hours and listened to somebody who is dry speak about a subject, whereas you go to another church and they make humor, or light of certain things, and you continue to go back.*

(Jesus)   So, I was not trying to be funny. I was not attempting to make everybody laugh, but they did. When the spirit emerges and overrides the human consciousness that is where the fun begins.

60

(Peter and John)

Scribes

Joe: Jesus, were the scribes always following these authors of the New Testament around because they wanted to be closer to understanding who you were? Or were they hired?

(Jesus) No, they did not follow around, but each town that we would go to, there would be scribes. There are a couple scribes within the group that could write, read, but there were others that could not do this. There were others that could write just as the authors wrote, but the scribes would write more intricately and put the words down in a formal fashion.

(Peter and John)

Parable of the Radio and Hard Drive

Joe: *I sure am glad Jesus can be everywhere at the same time. I feel so guilty taking his time.*

(Jesus) *Why do you feel guilty?*

Joe: *I don't know. I'm thinking of the church today and they brought up that story again how everyone wants your attention... how in the world can you accommodate everyone that wants your attention at the same time?*

(Jesus) *I am in each human being. Everything that I have ever done and everything that I will ever do is stored within your body and within your soul and it is too hard for some human minds to understand this, but this is stored within you. For there is no time, there is no time on this side so everything is happening at once. And by each person having a piece of me inside of them, every single person has a copy of that which they may access at any time.*

Joe: *So we have you inside of us, and inside of you is the Holy Spirit? Or is the Holy Spirit separate and you separate inside of me? plus my spirit too? It's kind of crowded inside there.*

Marisa: There are a lot of heavenly bodies inside us. There is the physical body and there are all the energetic bodies. Humankind knows of 12, but there are several more. There are 67 in fact. And these all carry out into different pieces of the universe and they each carry information……Here is Eden (One of Joe's Guides)....

(Eden) They each carry information that is pertinent to living a lifetime on the earth plane or other physical planes. As you learn to develop each one of these bodies and as you begin to learn to communicate with these bodies, you see that, we see that, and we try to have the world see that, we are all one. This word is used... this term is used so loosely. People say "we are all one, we are all one, we do not disintegrate, we stand together, we are all one," but nobody truly gets the understanding that we really are all one. Because we each are all made of the same thing and what we are made of, we have that inside of us, that pure peace inside of us, just as a daughter has her father's energy within her, if she was able to communicate with that energy, then that daughter would be able to know everything that he knew. This is a lot of the information that is stored in DNA. But human beings are only first starting to begin to understand DNA.

Marisa: Here's Jesus with another parable ....

Parable of the Radio and the Hard Drive

(Jesus) So in saying that the Holy Spirit is in each person, you may look at that as one little two-way radio. You look at the Christ light as another little radio. You can look at the human spirit as another radio. You can look at the soul, the over soul, you can look at the guides, all as different radios, and when one wants to communicate with one of these things, the radio buzzes the spirit

incarnation in which they want to communicate with, and that spirit talks, therefore the vibration is affected by the person who is asking for help. And in asking for help, each person could ask 15 different questions and everybody would get a different answer at the same time. For if everything you knew, Joe, if every single thing you knew was on a hard drive, so to speak, if everything you ever knew and everything you ever will know, and people had a key to that hard drive stored inside of them, that they could access at any time, just by asking a question, they would receive an answer from the abundant amount of information that is stored within your hard drive. Does this make sense?

Joe: Sort of. So, basically Jesus is comparing himself to like a hard drive but we're not really smart enough yet to know how to tap into all of that knowledge?

Marisa: Yes. Here is Eden. She wants to clarify ....

(Eden) *As the world evolves into the fourth and higher dimensions, everybody will be able to communicate with that divine piece inside of them, and that is why many other planets have the ability to tap into this divine piece inside of them and therefore they remember who they are. They incarnate only to develop their abilities, to live in different places, to learn from the people, to learn different healing modalities, different cultures, but living on the earth plane you're correct, many do not have the ability to accept that they have Christ within them, even if they are a Christian.*

Joe: Jesus has said that 85% of self-proclaimed Christians are really skeptical and find it hard to believe in him because in today's world of science coupled with a 2000-year-old and hard to understand Bible, Christians find it hard to put trust in something and someone they can't see or hear.

Marisa: I'm glad I can see and hear him.

Joe: You're lucky!

62

(Peter and John)

Is it Evil to Hear Your Voice?

Joe: *An Elder from my Sunday morning church read our book and really thinks it is evil because of what we're doing. And the Bible is filled with passages that say do not seek out mediums, yet the prophets would see angels of the Lord, and they would have dreams. And my understanding is that through these visitations and dreams they were truly communicating with the other side like Marisa. Is this evil what we are doing, Jesus? Seriously, is this forbidden (what we're doing with you)?*

(Jesus)   This is not forbidden in that one has the discernment between good and evil. One has the discernment when one is communicating with this side, with the mal-intent to hurt someone else, this is bad. (Unfortunately) there are many that use their communication lines with this side against others for their own gain. This is not evil and we do not like to use the term "evil" or "good." For it is all placed in the hands of man what these things are. As the world evolves and more and more people hear us on this side and hear us in these higher dimensions, it will become more normal. It is already becoming more normal. And it was normal back in the Biblical days. Many people heard spirits, but there was a lower conscious level, so the spirits in which they heard and saw were of a much lower nature. So, understand that.

Joe: As long as we continue to do this to uplift people, to understand you, Jesus, and to understand Christ, and to understand God and the Holy Spirit, then it's okay to talk to you?

(Jesus) Absolutely. It is okay for anybody to talk to me. For people hear my voice all the time. But then we fall back to what we've just discussed before, the unworthiness, just as you have said, Joe, you feel unworthy to speak with me, but if you look at me and the information in which I am giving you as something that is more of a storage of information, then you are in fact drawing from that information and sharing it with others that do not have that ability. Or that do not believe they are worthy of it.

Joe: Well right now when I try to.... actually my friends believe what I tell them. Its people in general, acquaintances that think that what we are doing is very, very wrong, and......

Marisa: By talking to Jesus? Or by talking to angels? By talking to dead people?

Joe: By talking to all of the above, everybody that you just mentioned; people who have passed on, our guides, our angels, you Jesus. Nobody believes that we're actually talking to you because everybody, everybody wants to hear your voice, everybody wants to hear your voice. I mean, they talked about it again at church. If you were there, which you said you were, then you heard them sing it in worship again tonight...."We all want to hear your voice, Jesus"....

(Jesus) And everybody does hear my voice. But they just do not recognize it, for my voice sounds like your thoughts. My voice does not come through in booming stereo speakers. It comes

Book V   Ask Jesus

through as a whisper in your head, or the sound of your own thoughts, so when the sound of your thoughts come in, and they are different from what you are used to, and you have called me in, then this is what you will hear. There are just others like your daughter, like yourself, that are willing to step out and say that there is a communication here, even though the both of you will be ridiculed. But by those who do not ridicule, they will learn and they will see.

Joe: I'm looking forward to that. Let me ask one more --.

Marisa: *Looking forward to ridicule?*

Joe: No, I'm not looking forward to the ridicule. I'm looking forward to being able to stand up to it and then know that there are people that will be helped by what we're doing.

Marisa: *Yeah!*

63

(Peter and John)

Forgiveness

Joe: This bothers me a lot, Jesus, really, and I'm sure if it bothers me, it bothers everybody, and that is we are told to ask for your forgiveness for our sins. If those sins linger in our heads, then we can't seem to feel worthy enough to accept the fact that you forgive us and so we keep asking for forgiveness over and over and over again for the same stupid things that we did that we are remorseful for. How do we shake that out of our head? How do we get that out of our head? How do we finally come to the realization that you do forgive us for the stupid things we've done?

(Jesus) When you stop looking at it as "I" am forgiving you, and look at it as "You" are forgiving you, for as your guide so eloquently put it, we are all one. For when you look at yourself as a piece of me and you're asking for forgiveness, you are truly just releasing negative energies from your, as you say, "Snow globe." You are releasing these negative energies because you say "I am done with these. They are not mine anymore. This is gone." So the

reason why people hold onto these things is because, just as we have just said, they feel unworthy. And there is no recognition, nothing is shown to them that is tangible that says "Good job for asking for forgiveness, you passed, you're approved." So, one must just truly believe that they are forgiven, and understand that when living on the earth plane, when living in physicality, mistakes are made. Mistakes are made, indeed. So when you ask how you forgive yourself for things that you have done, you do not even need to ask, so to speak, you just know that I have already forgiven you.

Joe: I really appreciate that. Now I have to convince my own ego and mind.

(Christ) For I have known everything that you do, for everything is recorded within the Holy Spirit, within I, Christ. Everything that is ever done or will be done has been recorded within your energy field. For you truly are -- and I do not mean this literally -- like your own universe. You carry within you the knowledge of every universe ever made by God. You carry this within your body. You carry everything of mine within your body. You carry the secrets and the mysteries of the universe within your body. So how could you technically be a sinner when sin is experienced to grow, lessons are experienced to grow, and many times souls come to the earth plane so that they can experience this.

Joe: That sounds like we're programmed to sin.

(Jesus) To clarify this, you must understand that we are all divine beings, divine beings of God, and as we incarnate in the earth plane, we are incarnating into bodies, into minds that by definition is called sin; for the sin is that which is against God, *against the divine nature of that which is spirit. For there are many things that human beings will call sin that aren't truly sin, and other things that some beings will not call sin that truly are sin. So understand and know that this is a very loosely termed word, for there are many different definitions for it by many different people. But when we speak of this and we say of this that souls incarnate on the earth plane to experience sin to grow, this is true, this is true. Do not think of sin as of the devil, of Lucifer. Think of sin as being human. And this is not to say that human beings are true sin, but there is a duality between light and not-light on the earth plane, and if human beings were to only experience, only experience the divinity within, and only to experience the light, they might as well stay on this side. So know that when they say 'ask for forgiveness', way back in the days, asking for forgiveness was for a priest.*

Joe: That's right. They had to go to a priest.

(Jesus) *You would go to ask them for forgiveness so that they could then ask me for forgiveness, and then they would get paid. But know that before you even think a thought, we have already heard it. Before you even speak a word, we have heard it. So if you are thinking "God please forgive me," it has already been done. So you must release the past, you must not feel guilty for the past otherwise you will carry that guilt within your field and only attract guilty natured people.*

Joe: Well, the sins though that we commit, we hurt other people. Even asking them for forgiveness, that's few and far between. There're a lot of people that get hurt .....

(Jesus) *This is all part of the human experience. For when one is hurt, they learn and when one is not hurt, they learn. But this is part of the human experience and this is part of the risk that souls take when being incarnated onto earth.*

Book V   Ask Jesus

64

(Peter and John)

Parable of the Baby Monitor

Joe: *So no one is ever alone?*

(Jesus)   You may look at it like a baby sleeping with a baby monitor. The baby is sleeping and everything is fine. Nobody worries. But they hear the baby cry and they go run. They don't just run to the monitor. They run to the room. So look at it like that. Know that each person is protected but they are not spied on, or watched. Each person has access to an army of angels and because each person has the knowledge of Christ, the knowledge of the Holy Spirit within their body, technically we are all mini gods, so to speak, because we have access to that information and we can co-create with the divine creator a life that we desire and in that

come the ability to connect to those that we love on one side or another. So in answer to your question, it depends on what each soul has decided they want to do. If one goes to a concert and they choose "I'm going to take three friends with me so that I don't get lost within this crowd" and another says, "I'm just going to go with one person" or "I'm going to go by myself but I have my cell phone just in case something happens, I can call someone." So everybody is completely different. So for the most part, each person has anywhere between 5-7 teachers, guides or family members that are with them at all times and this includes angels.

Joe: Whoa....okay....so like when I went to church tonight I'm going to guess there's lots and lots and lots of teachers, guides, angels, family members, etcetera in the church with us tonight then....

(Jesus) Absolutely. You can look at it like this. You can look at it as they are actually on the earth plane, or they are communicating through the telephone. There are many times where family members including your mother or your father, will come in and technically they are somewhere else, but they are dialing in.... technically they are calling in from another place. You are seeing them just like a photograph telephone. You are seeing the words in action and they are becoming a manifestation of those words. There are other times where we actually come to the earth plane and that can be itself much greater, with the ringing of the ears, the tapping of the head, the chills on the body. Many times this is when we make our entrance into the earth plane. But yes, in church, there are many who are receiving downloads, so to speak, information from their higher self. The higher self is always receiving information from the guides from this side.

Book V   Ask Jesus

65

(Peter and John)

Who Created Christ?

Joe: *Well, now may be the perfect time to ask Jesus, then, the question that I posed earlier: does Jesus' higher self look at the Holy Spirit like a person like we look at Jesus as a person? Or does Jesus look at the Holy Spirit as just a consciousness?*

(Jesus)   We are all energy. We are all energy. I do not look at myself as a person. I do not even look at you as people. I look at you as consciousness. I look at you as souls. I look at you as intelligence. I look at you as energy living within creatures that are human. For each energetic being on this side, each energetic being on that side are all just that -- energy, consciousness, awareness. And yes, yes, the Holy Spirit I see as a being, a being

of light. I would call it a being of light, a being of light of that which each and every being of light has been created from, created from indeed. For as you look at this being of light, this being of light, you will see that different shards of this being have been taken and put into each being that it has created, that it has created indeed. And as these beings of light with this – as Christians call the Holy Spirit – each of these beings of light having this inside of them enter into human beings, animalistic beings, beings in other worlds, beings in other planets, each being still has a light being within it. So in answer to your question I would call the Holy Spirit, as you call, a light being, just as you are a light being.

Joe: So the Holy Spirit can be considered as a – well, as one spirit with personality?

(Jesus) Yes, one being with personality, yes.

Joe: Okay. So Jesus does see the Holy Spirit as a being.

Marisa: Absolutely.

Joe: And that being has taken little pieces of himself and stuck them into every single human. Not just every human but every single soul.

Marisa: Every created being.

Joe: That's right. The Holy Spirit created everything including Christ, right? Who created Christ?

(Jesus) The Holy Spirit.

Joe: The Holy Spirit and God together? Or Just the Holy Spirit?

(Jesus)   *Just the Holy Spirit.*

66

(Peter and John)

Must you be Christian to have Christ?

Joe: *It just bothers me that devout Christians and pastors condemn anybody that does not accept Jesus Christ as their savior.*

(Jesus)   *Well, this has been going on for years. No one can expect it to change unless there are missionaries, warriors, to enter into the earth plane that are old souls, like the two of you, to bring truth to wisdom, truth to the history, wisdom to knowledge; and as each person begins to understand that the church is government, they will begin to see that the simplistic are accepting God,*

accepting the light, accepting that within you and thereby using the information that is within. But each person needs to accept this in a different way and some people need to be told. But the criticism, the judgment, the killing, the non-acknowledgment of peoples other than the Christians has been happening since the Christians fought against the Jews to say that I was god, whereby everyone is god. So understand that this began as a fight. Christianity began as a fight and it continues and there are many who will trademark themselves as someone who must be a Christian even if they don't believe thereby allowing people to criticize them so that they may then feel bad for themselves, and then think "oh God must have mercy on me because people are so mean to me."

(Eden)   So there are a lot of head games going on, so to speak, on the earth plane, and there are many people who play head games with themselves.

Marisa: That was Eden. She's jumping in but here's Jesus ....

(Jesus)   As soon as everybody understands that the life that I carry -- the life that we carry -- is much stronger than the light that the earth plane can handle, that's when human beings will begin to come to....(inaudible). Four percent of the world is acknowledging that Christ is within them without having to be Christian.

Marisa: And he's saying ....

(Jesus)   "I'm not the only way to God. There are many incarnations of Christ."

Joe: But those.... That is exactly what Jesus said though, when he was man, when he was there on the earth. Those words are in red in the Book of John where he says "I am the way, I am the *truth, I am the life and no one gets to the father but through me." Those are Jesus' exact words.*

(Jesus)   Communication is not the issue, it's raising one's vibration and that to be able to hear and communicate with the Father, so to speak. But the Father is within each. The mother is within each. And Christ is within each. And each person can communicate with those pieces inside of them, for they are them. They are God, the mother, the father, Christ. This is each person. So as one raises their vibration energetically and the world raises their vibration, the next on the line to speak would be Christ other than the higher self. And one evolves and becomes Christed; that is going to Christ first. But the misunderstanding is that one must go to Christ even if they don't believe in Christ to get to the Father. For one has a higher self and one has guides that can be a conduit for communication with the other side. One may choose to come down to be an atheist, for they were a priest in a past life. This does not mean that they cannot communicate with God. The spirit within is that which must communicate...

Marisa: This is Jesus. The higher self of Jesus.

(Jesus)   The spirit within the human body is that which must communicate with the Christ to evolve, to evolve into communication with the Father, or going home, so to speak. So it is the spirit within. So even if the human mind does not remember, the spirit remembers. And the higher self and those left on the other side remember. And the angels, the angels specifically take those prayers straight to God.

67

(Peter and John)

Multi-dimensionality

Joe: Just out of curiosity, this question is for Jesus.... did you explain or teach about the Father and the astral realms, the etheric realms, the different layers of dimensions that we all pass through to your apostles? Or was that just too much for them to handle at that time?

(Jesus) I explained the multi-dimensionality in a way that they could understand. I told them that there were many worlds, many mansions, many places in which the human spirit or the soul resides all at the same time, and as they are in their earthly bodies

learned to communicate with the higher aspects, the ones living within the higher mansions, they may draw that knowledge from that mansion and pull it into their earthly life. So they understood this and I preached about it, but much of this has been lost in translation and much of this has been lost, for the church does not understand how there could be more worlds for a soul to live in, other than this world that you can see with your five senses.

Joe: So basically, the counsel -- and I don't remember the official name of the counsel that was with Constantine, but I'm going to guess they weren't a real high level. So they were doing the best they could to bring together Christians and they wanted a book. But according to Paul, they had 222 epistles, of which they used 27. The rest of them are wherever.

(Jesus) Correct. This is correct and this is a magical number, so to speak. This is a number that explains totality and oneness and brings everyone together. There were many, many books that they reviewed, but many, many more that were written that have never been found. There have been stone that has been carved into by many, many of those that I knew so that they would not forget the lessons which were taught.

Joe: So have those stone tablets or walls been found by anybody?

(Jesus) Some of them have. Twenty percent of them have. The other 80% are either buried or somewhere where there is not access to them, but they still reside where they were prior to the earth shifting.

68

(Peter and John)

The Return of Jesus

Joe: It says in the Bible that we're not supposed to know Jesus' return.

(Jesus) And the curiosity is good and the evolution of man is good. And the understanding and asking what will be happening is fine, but having trust and faith in that when I say that I am returning, it is because each person is evolving to the point where they are truly harnessing and manifesting in their life as if they were me. For they are evolving and a new world is created because each person is able to live, not just as their spirit living in a human body, but live as Christ living in a human body.

Marisa: He's saying that he's returning through....

Book V   Ask Jesus

Joe: I don't want to know. He says that we will never know. We won't know the hour, we won't know the day, and he will come as a breeze in the night. He's going to come when we totally, totally least expect it. But then again, that's the way the Jews were too. The Jews were like, "We want our David, we want our ruler, we want our warrior!"

Marisa: He's not physically coming back. It's through……

Joe: Marisa, tell him please, don't tell me anything there.

Marisa: Why?

Joe: Because I am not going to detract anything from the Bible. I don't want to take any……

Marisa: …. you can tell me, Jesus.

Joe: I don't want to take anything away from people's faith.

Marisa: Okay. He's just saying that basically he's going to come back in each person. Each person is going to have access to all of his knowledge and be able to do what he does and more, and that in itself is him coming back in everyone.

69

(Peter and John)

Peter and Jesus are Funny Together

Joe: *Jesus, how do you feel when people stub their toe and it hurts so badly, and they blurt out... "Jesus Christ!"... Does that bother you?*

(Jesus) *Absolutely not! Human beings are human beings and their intention is not that they are yelling at me. They are just saying this. It is a way of speaking.*

Joe: *So you don't take it negatively?*

(Jesus) *I do not take anything negatively, for I am not human.*

Book V   Ask Jesus

Joe: Okay. Gotcha.

(Jesus)   Humans are defensive and humans are......

Joe: You don't feel we're taking your name in vain then?

(Jesus)   No. No.

Joe: Okay. Actually that's kind of good. I mean, it keeps his name out in the forefront because his name is always, you know, any time anybody hurts themselves or something weird happens, they say, "Jesus Christ!" They don't say in Jesus' name. They just say "Jesus Christ!"

Marisa: Yeah. I wonder how that started.

Joe: I don't know. It just started. Everybody......

Marisa: Peter just said, "Look at me." He stubbed his toe and he went, "Jesus Christ!" Jesus looked over and said, "Yes?"

Joe: Now that's funny!! There is humor. There really is.

Marisa: Oh my gosh. Peter and Jesus are funny.

70

(Peter and John)

I'm a victim. Is this all there is?

Joe: This example would work for anyone with a permanent disability or hopeless relationship. My friend Gene's condition became permanent following a stroke and her normal way of life was over. Her question was "Jesus, is this my plan? This is awful." I wrote back to her saying...'

Marisa: No, listen. This is Yeshua.

(Yeshua)   As we bring forth truth and as we bring forth the honor and the messages that we bring through, we bring these with love, we bring these with joy, and we bring these with peace.

Book V   Ask Jesus

(Jesus to Gene)   Dear child, as we bring this message to you, we bring it with love, hope and peace and joy. We bring this to you to faithfully and give to you the hope, the hope of a new generation, the hope of a new life. There are many energies that are brought upon one when they do not believe in themselves. For when they do not believe in themselves, when they do not stand tall, this is something that they bring upon, they bring upon (themselves) indeed. This is not to say that anybody has done anything wrong. This is not to say that anybody has not moved forward in their life trying to do the best that they can do. But as human beings, even I as a human being, we are programmed, we are programmed to think things, do things, feel things, and just accept and allow people to do things to us.

For when one feels as if they are a victim, when one feels as if life is taking them and doing with them what life wants to do, one will attract and allow people around them to victimize them. For even if somebody is not a victimizer, energetically being brought into the field of someone who feels as if they are a victim, for any circumstance, and this is generally speaking, and on this account as well, for when one feels as if they are a victim, they will make the other the victimizer thus driving them away or, keeping them in the picture.

So please understand. Please understand as we come in here now, we come in and we place you in charge of your life. For when you ask "is this how I will be for the rest of my life?" this is a question that you must answer. This is a question that you must see. This is a question that you must know within your heart is true because if you do not want this to be, it will not be. If you are comfortable in feeling this way because this is how you have felt for so long, then this is how you will allow yourself to continue feeling. But this is a breaking point you see. For you're asking this question, you're reaching out to something that is outside of yourself, that is outside of your mind, for your mind is deceitful to you on so many levels and this is because you have been hurt.

You have been hurt. But this hurt has come into your life and it has surrounded you. So you continue to allow yourself to be hurt. This is a cycle. This is a cycle, dear child. And as you come in and you release these cycles and you see that you have complete control over your life, you have complete control over what you want to do and you will truly see. You will truly see that your life will not be like this unless you allow it, unless you allow it indeed. For when you break free of these patterns, and you break free of the convoluted thoughts that as a human being we are stuck in "what God dealt us", so to speak, this is when the human being can take control and ascend past the menial thoughts that the third dimensional egoic qualities bring in.

For these are in essence, as I see, these are the qualities of the dark side. The mind brings in the qualities of the dark side. So as you ascend past these voices in your head which are in your own head telling you that you are worthless, telling you that you are nothing, telling you that in order to be in somebody's life you must let them do whatever they want regardless of how horrible it makes you feel and how horrible they know it makes you feel, but continue to do this then this is something that, as you begin to love yourself, as you begin to see yourself as the you that you want to be, you will see that if your vibration raises, that you will not see that this is okay and things will change, things will change. This is all we must say.

So please know that you are loved. Know that you are loved genuinely and deeply. Know that you are a child, a child of God, and we know that you know this. We know that you know this indeed. But as you begin to accept and allow people to love you, as you allow people and you allow them and you let the love in, you will allow it to fill you.

For many, many years you have shut down your heart so that you do not allow the love in. And now (of all things) you've shut your heart, you've shut your heart to us as well. So please, make it a daily intention, make it a daily intention to ask us to open your heart so that you may feel the love of the Creator, feel the love of the angels that surround you, for you have angels that surround you at all times. It is not because they have pity on you, it is not because they feel sorry for you, it is because they want to be here. They have asked you if they can be here and you have agreed.

So please begin to take the stance of being strong and knowing what you want and moving forward and ask us for that help. Ask us for that help indeed, because you are a true warrior. You are a true warrior indeed. And if you knew and remembered who you truly are, you would not be asking this question. You would be taking charge and if you do not know what you want, we will just call you human because no human really knows what they want. So ask me, just say each day, "Will you help me open my heart? I don't know how, but I'm here so please help." That's all you have to say. That's all you have to say. And you will begin to feel the vibration of love surrounding you and knowing that you are exactly where you need to be and exactly ready to make those changes. I love you, dear child.

71

(Peter and John)

Prayer

(Jesus)   *We hear people's prayers every day. We hear the people pray: "I must have that red car, but I hate red cars. God, get me that red car. But I really hate red cars. God I want a yellow car. Please God, please, please, please, a yellow car. Oh but actually I don't like yellow cars either."*

So many human beings will go through life and they will say, "I want something, but never mind, I don't want that, I'm not worthy, I'm not worthy. Oh I want that black sports car. Oh, but never mind, God, I'm not worthy. I'm evil, I'm bad. But never mind, don't give it to me."

So this is something that human beings must work on. This is something that human beings must see, that when you ask for something, you're asking because you want it. You do not follow it up with "but only if I'm worthy." Because you will know, you will know that when you feel worthy and you ask for things, you will receive them. It is the way the energy works. It is the way the particles spin. It is the way that the quantum electricity works within the earth plane. And we will not get too deeply into the atomic structure, so to speak, but understanding that this is all science, this is all science unexplained. And as you see that positive attracts negative, and these neurons surround the different thought patterns in which you bring in, you will see that your thoughts are action. So ask and ye shall receive. We will be here for you. I am here for you for you are a true believer. You are a true love of mine and I am here for you.

Joe: Is that Jesus?

Marisa: Yeah. It was Yeshua Ben Joseph.

72

(Peter and John)

Advice to Pastors and Teachers

Joe: Rosemary *(who was introduced in Matthew and Mark's interviews) described Jesus as having a good sense of humor and that he liked people to be happy and laughing. On the contrary the Bible depicts him to be so dour, so sad and so serious. Everything was so serious. Now we know he was serious for he had to be serious but was he also playful? Was he also humorous? How did he keep people's attention if he was so dour?*

(Jesus) *Humor and joy are important tools for success. When you go to a church to hear pastors speak, when you go to a church in these modern days, do you understand what the pastor says during the sermon when Scripture is dryly read? Or do you remember what they say when they are joyous and they truly believe and understand and take those words and put them into their own words and give joyful examples to where you laugh so*

that later on you may not remember the Scripture but you remember the example and you remember laughing so this brings back the memory and therefore, somewhere inside (of you) you're remembering Scripture.

This is just as when you are in a schooling room. When you are in a schooling room, and there is a schooler [teacher]: There is a teacher who may sit up in front of the class and read the education to the children and some will be able to understand it, or the teacher may stand and pace and become more animated and the children will remember the animation, therefore remembering what the teacher was saying while animated. This is not to say that I was a goof-ball but humor ....

Marisa: Abraham leaned over and went "goof-ball"....

(Jesus)   *... this does not mean that I was a goof-ball so to speak. This does not mean that I was a town idiot, so to speak. This just meant that I was bringing joy to the world. I was bringing peace to the world for this was what I was bringing into my existence just as you two are bringing this into existence. For people are bored by dry words. People are bored by somebody telling them what to do. When one can show: "Look at how I feel, look at what I am doing," and people want to be like that, and that person explains, just as this channel explains in the classes in which she teaches, "I am this way and I am that way, and I feel this way, and sometimes I feel this way, and sometimes I feel this way." People can relate to the "I feel this way and I feel this way." Therefore, as opposed to the channel saying "You must read your vibration by meditating perfectly" this is not the way that people learn. People learn by being engaged in a teacher and this is what I brought. I brought an example; I brought an example of what I had learned, what I had learned indeed, from the Father; what I* *had brought in and understood through days and days and years and days and days and weeks and months and years of meditating, or as you say, praying, in bringing in this vibration and raising the vibration and activating all that is energetic within the human body, nobody truly understands the dynamic of how the human body can relate to that which is spirit as you two have intended to call it. So, please understand that when I was teaching these lessons I would bring in the joy, I would bring in the examples and now I'm your teacher and have schooled you. So, this is how I dealt with it when I was on the earth plane, and this is how I still deal with it here in the ethers, still remaining on the earth plane, but just unseen.*

Joe: So, on the other side there's happiness and laughter just like there is in this world?

(Jesus) Absolutely. That's all there is.... joy and happiness.

Joe: Oh. I'm picturing his 12 disciples. From what I understand there're about 4 of them that don't get a lot of press, so to speak, since they were more like body guards, kind of keeping the crowds back and not really being teachers. So I kind of think of them as not the brightest bulbs in the store. I can see how they would ask silly questions that everybody else would think is silly, but Jesus would have to explain it anyway. So I'm seeing Jesus doing it with humor and the other disciples, not laughing at their friends but laughing with them in a way that they would learn, would still learn together.

(Jesus) My disciples understood the way the energy worked. My disciples understood that we were all the same in activating the Holy Spirit or activating the central meridian of that which is the central nervous system in equation with the energetic system that it surrounds. When activating that within the human *body, connecting into Source, so to speak, one is bringing about many abilities, many as people say today, spiritual abilities that human beings do not quite understand. All of the men and women who walked with me had these activations and then being around others who had a higher vibration, were all channels; channels of, as you say, your higher self or as you say, the Divine. They became channels. For many of them, many of them were much smarter than they could ever imagine. Things would just come out of their mouths and we found that very, very hilarious. We would laugh and say, "Where did that come from, oh Nehemiah?"*

Marisa: Who's Nehemiah? Where did that come from, oh Nehemiah?

Joe: I don't know. There were hundreds of disciples. Maybe that was an expression back then like us saying "Jesus Christ" all the time today when something happens or maybe he was a goofy one of the unknown prophets.

(Jesus) And we would listen, we would listen to the words that came through, for I am not the only one that speaks of, as humans say, the Father. I am not the only one. Everybody does. It is equating the physical body into a clear channel that is fully activated and (then) connect with that which is the Father, that which is the spirit, the soul and every level in between. This is when the human being becomes full. This is when the human being becomes a whole in that the human being is spirit. The human being is of God. The human being is Christ. So please know that all of these disciples were working toward this and eventually through a lifetime, became what they intended for they were all bright souls. But many had many different upbringings, and as you say, not the smartest. But this did not change the spirit for there are many, many on the earth plane at this time that are not smart at all.

Many of the problems that we had in getting through to this channel is there is intelligence, and this intelligence blocks much of what we say because the mind can speak faster than us and this may be hard to believe because we do speak fast but understand that the mind can sometimes be a channel's worst enemy.

Joe: I believe that.

Marisa: Who's Nehemiah?

Joe: I don't know. It's probably just an expression. I like his examples of how to teach effectively though. Jesus is so smart.

73

(Peter and John)

Parable of the Mannequin

Joe: Has the Holy Spirit always been within mankind? And why was it so – why does the Bible make it seem like the Holy Spirit did not exist until the day of Pentecost which was the resurrection of Jesus?

(Jesus)   The way that men see things, the way that man sees things in general is that things are on the outside and brought to the inside and being activated. They do not look at it as.... look at it like this ....

Parable of the Mannequin

(Jesus)   Inside the human body ... look at the human body as a hollow mannequin. Imagine that there are many light bulbs inside of that mannequin. There are many things. And, there's a light bulb that symbolizes the Holy Spirit. When this light bulb is turned on or activated, this light shines brightly and it fills the entire mannequin; this light begins shooting out of the mannequin's head and out of the mannequin's feet, therefore connecting this mannequin to the Divine, to the Divine as to Mother Earth.

By understanding that when one is connected in these ways then the vibration in which they have is raised. The higher the vibration of a human being and the etheric subtle and energetic bodies that this spirit is residing in, or this consciousness resides in, the higher the vibration, the more quote-unquote "spiritual abilities" one will have. These are called spiritual abilities because these are all things that spirits can do even when in a human body. But when they say that the Holy Spirit comes to – comes to – a man, they are in essence saying that the mannequin does not have the light bulb in there to begin with, and somebody comes and puts it in the mannequin. This is not the case. It is there and it is activated. It is activated indeed. The switch has just not been turned on.

So when one turns that switch on of, as they say, the Holy Spirit, or one turns on that switch of the 'I Am', or the 'I Am Divine', or the 'I Am God'....when they turn that belief on and understand that they are the true co-creator with the Creator of their life, the vibration that they carry raises. Heaviness falls away. And yes, spiritual abilities are developed. Does this answer the question?

Joe: Yeah. I love his examples... his parables. Okay, so I'm picturing that people just didn't realize they had the Holy Spirit within them until Jesus said to them: "I am going to give you the Spirit of Truth and that will be your helper." And the spirit of truth therefore is my angel light bulb within.

(Jesus) The Spirit of Truth is technically what people, man, call the Holy Spirit. The Spirit of Truth is within each and every person. And just as we have spoken in many other sittings that we have had, we have mentioned the hollowed out tennis balls (example is found with interviews with Matthew, Mark and Luke).

We have mentioned these because each one represents a different layer, a different aspect, a different piece of that human being. So if you look at the totality of the consciousness of what a spirit really contains, you can look at that mannequin and you can look at that light bulb, and technically that is the Holy Spirit, but there may be another bigger light bulb on the outside of it that is the soul's personality, another light bulb that is the spirit personality, and a big huge light bulb up in the mannequin's head with a big, red beaming light, that is the intellectual mind and it says "I am you, I am you, I am you," with strobe lights and red lights going off. And only until the consciousness of that mannequin -- which lies in the belly and in the heart -- as their consciousness realize that the big red flashing thing in their head is technically just a tool they may turn that off and allow the white light inside of them to take over the consciousness.

Book V   Ask Jesus

74

(Peter and John)

Parable of the Human Suit

Joe: That's great. I love it. And, I'll talk to Peter, when we have a chance to talk to Peter again....

Marisa: *Here is Peter again on the "human clothing" the "human suit" ...*

Parable of the Human Suit

(Peter) *And when we say that the Holy Spirit is within each person, many people call the Holy Spirit different things. You call it the Holy Spirit. We call it the Light. We call it the Eternal. We call it the Alpha, the Omega. We call it the Infinite. So understanding that the brightest possible light that can be placed within a human being is that of the Holy Spirit, as you call it, that each person has this divine fire, this divine flame inside and it is ready to be activated. It does not have to be through, as humans say, Christianity. It does not have to be through a certain religion. This can be done through meditation or prayer. This can be done through self-affirmation. This can be done through the realization that you are a divine being living in a human suit.*

You are living in a body and this body is like clothing that talks. And as you begin to see that this clothing is talking you realize the talking clothing is not you. It is something you are wearing. And as you and other human beings become aware that this talking clothing really doesn't know much of what it's saying, and you begin to realize that it is just your clothing talking, that is when the vibration raises. That is when one begins to realize "I am a spirit. I am God. I am love, and I am ascending into Christhood just as many others have with the help of those like me who have ascended as well."

Marisa: *I picture a bunch of talking clothes.*

Joe: *How do they come up with this stuff?*

Book V   Ask Jesus

75

(Peter and John)

Denying Christ

Joe: *I never thought of it that way. That is really a good lesson for today; that all of us are Peters. We have all denied Christ at one time or another.*

(Peter) Every day, every day. Everybody does every day. Every day that one doubts him or herself, he or she is then doubting that they are the divine. They are doubting that Christ, or as you call it, the Holy Spirit, resides inside. But this is okay. This is okay. When one says, "I really, really, really want this job and this job will just bring me everything I've ever wanted, it will bring me the riches and it will bring me the houses, and it will bring me the women, and it will bring me everything that this man desires," and then the man says to himself, "Oh, but you're a failure." This man has just denied Christ.

The Christ within can have everything Christ wants because this is Christ's world. So this is not denying Christ by saying, "Oh Christ you are a horrible person and I hate you and I don't believe in you." But there is that piece of us inside of us that you must look at, and when you begin to believe that you cannot do something that you want to do, because you do not believe in yourself, this is in essence denying that divinity inside and not allowing the divine to take over, as Yeshua through Peter so patiently said, the "human suit".

Marisa: He went like this…..like he was hanging himself up on a hanger.

Joe: Well let me ask him, though, in actual existence, did he actually deny Christ, his involvement with Christ?

(Peter) Oh yeah, more than three times.

Joe: More than three times?

(Peter) Oh yeah.

Book V   Ask Jesus

76

(Peter and John)

"Break a leg"

(Jesus)   There is so much symbolism that was written into the Bible as you call it but it was written in different languages, it was written in different tongues, and as it became translated over

the years it would be like this.... "Oh Joe, you've got this great interview. Break a leg!".... but, two thousand years down the road it comes across as.... "I despise you, Joe, I hope your legs break before you get to your interview."

Joe: Okay, I understand.... something gets lost in the translation over time....

(Jesus)   This is how the Bible has come about. This is not a bad thing, but it is uncontrollable by deciding how it came about. So human beings created it and this is okay. This brings people to faith, but unfortunately, the acts of man can drive people away, because just as Peter was so eloquently putting it, many of the things written in the Bible brought fear and unworthiness as opposed to humility, honor, love and devotion to self. For the church, and this is not to demean the church in any way, for it has brought much, much to this plane, but the church chooses to stand between those and God. And only now, as the vibration of the planet raises, are the ministers, the apostles of this planet in all religions beginning to preach that we are all God. And this is how it was written. This is how it was written, but it has been translated as.... "if you come here and you give us your money, we will tell God that you are very sorry and then you can go back to your life." This is not how it was intended. This is just how it happened.

And this is how it happens on a lot of planets, quite honestly. This is how it happens with baby planets because the human being, or the inhabitants of that planet, begin to worship the teachers as opposed to becoming one of the teachers. But as the children grow they begin to realize this. This is like children. Children look upon their parents (as though) they are not people. They either worship them or they despise them. They want to be like them or they want to be nothing like them. So in their minds, their actions show that they are either like them or not like them, or maybe a combination between the parents. But as they grow up, they realize, "Oh, I'm a person just like them and I can choose who I want to be."

And this is how the planets evolve. They look at the teachers and they either want to do exactly as they are doing, or exactly opposite. And as the planet and the civilizations and the people, and the inhabitants, evolve, they realize "Oh, I'm the same thing as that teacher. They just know a little bit more than me but I can know that much and more."

So this is how earth is becoming. Earth is in its adolescence, so to speak. It is rebelling. But this is okay and this is what makes these times so exciting because the Earth is applying for college and deciding where to go to school.

77

(Peter and John)

The Military of God

Marisa: So Yeshua I'm going to ask you a question please. If I call you in, are you the person that I need to call on to remove *any.... like when people have demons on them, are you going to remove them for me?*

(Jesus) Absolutely I will. You will not see it as this though because you do not truly have faith in me yet. You do not have the faith, for the religious ties, the religious cords in which you have running through the circuitry in which you live, abound you from believing that you are truly, truly worthy. But you see, the angels are (the) military of God, and whether they believe in you or not, they have been assigned to help you. Whether you are a horrible person that deserves to be laying in a gutter dead, which is what a piece of you says, the angels still have to protect you because they have been assigned to protect you. But I, a man, I -- you see me as Christ and you see yourself as unworthy -- but you will continue to work with me as your guide just as you have been. And as the time moves along, as the time moves along into the future, you will truly see that you are worthy. You are worthy. Every aspect of you is worthy and everything that you have ever done in self, everything you are going through at this time, is all a piece of the puzzle that you, Abraham, and I have created. You will truly see this. But do not feel bad for not feeling worthy, for this is also a piece of the equation. For when you learn this and as you are learning this, you have been discipling to those who are feeling exactly the way that you feel. Please continue to do what you do. Bring about the laughter. Bring about the animation. And bring about the true spirit of that which you are -- God. Just as we all are. We bless you, young Child. Continue on. We love you.

Book V   Ask Jesus

78

(Peter and John)

Mutant Humans

(Peter)   The angels carrying three extra DNA strands within the etheric body that they require to be fulfilled within the angelic kingdom incarnated as human beings but by carrying these

extra DNA strands they are able to breed in the intelligence and the higher vibrational energies of that which is the angelic kingdom. For most human beings today carry the DNA of an angel. Most human beings on this planet, unless they are from other planets, are carrying the DNA of the angels in which incorporated themselves into this earth 81,210 years ago for there are many mutations and many things that were done in order to vanquish the humans that were not human from the earth plane. There were floods, there were earthquakes, there were fires, and these were things to get rid of the human beings that were mutated. So understand this in that there is a ruler of this world and there is one that watches over this world and you may look at it....

Marisa: Look at who, Yeshua?

(Peter) *.... you may look at it as a project. You may look at it as a blueprint. You may look at it as a company, if you will, and you see that there are many managers, there are many employees, and if you look at the human beings as customers, the souls as customers, and the souls as incarnating into these human beings, you will see that there are many employees and the owners of the company on the other side that are recruiting clients to come onto the earth plane and to inhabit it. There are recruiters both from the dark and the light side, for there is a true battle, so to speak, because there are many that would like the earth plane to stay three dimensional, would like the earth plane to stay within the ego, within the lines of good or bad. Good or bad, white or black, alpha-omega, tall-short....*

Marisa: They're going through like a ton of combinations. Hold on. Peter with a hat just came in.

(Peter) *Tall or short? Tall or short! Yeshua is here for now. He says look at it like this. He says, the earth is like --.*

Book V   Ask Jesus

Marisa: That was Peter, not Yeshua. Hold on. Yeshua, will you talk to me, please?

79

(Peter and John)

Parable of the Orange and the Parallel Universes

(Jesus)   Think of the earth as an orange so that you can understand that it is supple and ripe and ready to create in itself another earth, and when this earth carbon copies itself into another dimension, we will begin to see that everything that is happening

here is also happening there, and our consciousness is able to go from this over to that.

It is very hard for a human mind to understand and it is very hard for us to explain to you something that the mind cannot even fathom. But imagine this, you are on an experiment. You're in an experiment. And from that experiment come 11 other mirrored worlds that have the exact same thing happening but the consciousness is different so different things are played out in different ways. Whereby you see somebody walk in to get a job and here they are unhappy that they receive the job. On the other world they are excited that they got the job. The same things are happening, it is just different emotions, and when you see that, the difference between third dimensional and fourth dimensional and fifth dimensional emotional levels, you see that even though the life is exactly the same, it is lived completely different and it is experienced by the higher self and the essence of that which is the soul in many different ways.

For the spirit or the soul does not just experience three dimensional lives. The spirit is experiencing all dimensions in all worlds in all parallel universes in all realities in all ways of possibly doing something. For there is another world where you went left in this one, you went right in the other, and the essence of that which is your soul is experiencing that as well. So by excluding your soul, excluding the spirit, excluding the higher self from that which is your consciousness you are truly, truly not experiencing life at all. Whereby bringing in energies and knowledge from the higher dimensional "Yous" you are able to bring in knowledge that you would not have in this one due to the emotional stability of most human beings

Book V   Ask Jesus

80

(Peter and John)

Parable of the 12 Story Building

(Jesus)   When the angelic kingdom reigned upon the third dimensional world they were hoping to bring this into a world where they could incarnate on a regular basis for they were only

living in the fifth, sixth, seventh, and eighth worlds. They were not living in the lower world. And they wanted to have a physical experience. Whereby, this is what they did. This is what they did indeed in hoping to create their own world, their own world, for there were many, many that got wrapped into that which is the Luciferian rebellion in that one with much power decided that they did not want to do what the plan was. They wanted to mix it up. And this was a good idea to many, this was a good idea indeed to many, except for the ones that did not think that it was a good idea.

So understand that it was all done in good intentions and there are still those who believe that it was done with good intentions. They are still from the belief that there should be no reason why we have to evolve into combining with our higher self, combining with our spirit, combining with our soul and losing our individuality. There are those who believe that they want to be their individual self for eternity. And this is understandable in that we have free will. So know that the ones that are walking in the light, so to speak, are those who want to rejoin their consciousness with a group and lose their individuality and no longer be themselves.

(Jesus)   *When I say that some believed it to be a good idea, I do not rebuke this comment for there are many on the earth plane and many in the celestial realms and in the ethers that believe different things. What one must understand, what one must understand indeed is that, there are different beings at different levels of consciousness and when I speak of those who do not want to re-emerge, re-emerge with their higher self, I must explain this in a fashion in which you can understand.*

Parable of the 12 Story Building

(Jesus)   *For, when you look at a building, you look at a building, and you look at a building with 12 stories, you say "this is a person." So the building is a person. The person is not each floor. For if you look at the spirit being, the spirit being is the second floor and you look at the human being is the first floor. So when somebody says "I want to be the second floor forever. I want to be the second floor forever. I want to be my spirit forever and I want to live on the second floor forever," they are blind to the fact that they are already living on every single floor because they are the building. So when we say the spirit merges with the higher self, this is not truly, truly the way that it happens, for what happens is the awareness, the awareness of one's self begins to evolve just as we have talked prior to this about human beings deciding which consciousness, which level of awareness they want to plug into, so to speak.*

So, when we say this, we say this as there are many who get caught up in the illusion, the illusion that there are all these different floors in the building and forget that they are the building. They are the building. And by being the building they are still the first floor, the second floor, the third floor, the fourth floor. But the Luciferian rebellion is telling those that are on the second floor experiencing second floor life, saying, "Why would you ever want to be a third floor or a fourth floor or a fifth floor? Why would you ever want to do that? You would never be a second floor again." And so these aspects, these aspects of these buildings, these floors within these buildings, get caught up in being afraid that they are going to lose an entire segment of themselves. So when you look at yourself even by saying "Joe, when will I ever graduate to be my higher self?" You already are your higher self.

So as you begin to see that you are your higher self, and there are different aspects of you, different aspects of you that come into play at times, for Joe the human being is the first floor, and you may call up to the fifth floor and get some information, and you may call up to the second floor and get some information, up to the third floor and get some information, and get information from many different aspects of yourself, many different aspects of yourself, but it does not mean that you are not also those aspects. For what we must explain is sometimes the illusion is much more fun to souls than the real thing. For, the illusion, the illusion that we are separate, that we are separate from God is the game, is the game that we play. And we do not say it is a game because we belittle it. It is a game because it is something that people look at games as something that they want to win, they want to beat, they want to master.

81

(Peter and John)

Parable of the Golf Course Part II

(Jesus)   You look at your game of golf, Joe, look at each incarnation; each incarnation is a different day on the golf course. You will say, "Ooh, ooh, I got a bogie on hole 3 and I hit it into the

water and had to take an extra stroke. Next time I'm going to hit it a little bit to the left and that way it won't go in the water." And that's what you say in between games. And then the next game comes along and you're talking to your buddies, you're talking to your friends, and "oops" there it goes in the water again. You say, "Oh next time I'm not going to hit it in the water. I'm not going to hit it in the water." And look, there it goes in the water again. And that is how incarnation is over and over, the same mistakes, the same habits each soul has. Each soul has habit after habit and it's because of their energetic habits programming within yourself that says "must hit ball in water, must hit ball in water and take extra stroke" until one can realize, realize this is a game. I'm not programmed. I don't have to be programmed to hit it that way and I can say, "You know what? Even though I really want to hit it that way, I'm just going to hit it the other way."

So you must look at each incarnation and then also realize that when you go to hit that ball, you have up to 12 people standing behind you at any given time going, "Hey, hit to the left. Hit to the left. Don't hit it in the water." And it's your choice to choose if you want to hit the ball in the water or hit it the other way this time. So look at this life, this life on the earth plane as yes, there are the evils, there is the water where the ball can go into, but what fun would the game be without the sand traps and the water? This is the way that we look at the world. There must be something that defers us from the good, so to speak, to make it a challenge to stay within the good. And yes, there is suffering. Yes, there is violence. Yes, there is anger. Yes, there are many, many horrible, horrible things that souls must endure as human beings, but we all must remember that as souls living in human bodies, yes, humans are very real, humans are very real. But for souls we do not die. We live forever. We live forever. So, yes, there are horrible things happening, but there are many, many, many things to learn from these horrible things happening.

For if we were to place the world on a pedestal and say "there shall be no evil," souls would not want to incarnate here because they would get bored, they would not grow, they would not expand, they would not learn the amount that they would want to learn. So what you must see this as is a game; a very serious game. And each soul does not look at this like school. Each soul looks at this as a round of golf and says, "Next time I'm going to do better. Next time I'm going to get par. Next time I'm going to get a birdie. Next time..." And it's a challenge, and it's fun. And when they realize that they have the caddie and they realize that they have their buddies there that they couldn't see before that are helping them through to tell them which way to hit the ball, and how fast the wind is blowing, and which way to go, and which club to use, that is when, that is when the game gets really fun because no one else knows they have a caddie and no one else knows that they have someone to tell them which club to use.

So it's almost like there is a cheat sheet. And this is what I brought in. This is what I brought in as Jesus, as Jesus. I brought in the cheat sheet, the understanding that there is something inside that will direct you and tell you which way to go. And for those, those who get so angry at religion, they turn away from the fact that they have this help, that they have these angels, that they have this guidance, that they have this with them, that they have the whole course map right at their fingertips but they do not see this because they are trapped on the second floor, so to speak. They are trapped in the illusion that they are only one floor of their building. It would be like saying, "Hi, I am Joe," but it is only your leg speaking. It would be like your leg thinking that it is Joe. Or it would be like your hand thinking that it is Joe or even your brain thinking, "Hi, I am Joe." No, that's not the case. That's not the case. You are Joe. The whole vehicle is Joe. And your consciousness lives inside, and depending on which floor you choose to live on, that is the frequency, that is the consciousness and the awareness and the understanding of the universe that you bring in. If you choose to live on the top floor, this is your higher self, your soul, the highest possible piece of you, and you bring in, you bring in oneness. You bring in oneness. And this I say.

82

(Peter and John)

The Earth 'Grid' and the "Grand Experiment"

The Bible Speaks: Conversations with the New Testament Authors

(Jesus)   *"May I say something very quickly?" My brethren, my brother and my sister, I have not spoken with you in some time and I come to you, yes, as Jesus Christ as you've called me.*

Marisa: He's coming in like as the – not the human Yeshua – he's coming in as Jesus Christ.

(Jesus)   I come in today as I walked the earth with these men (the Authors), I walked the earth with the two of you not wearing the bodies in which you are wearing now, but we all walked the earth at the same time and brought in the frequencies of the earth at the same time. For all spirits that walk the earth at different times will have the same characteristics. They will have the same types of characteristics and they will have the same yearnings and wants for the earth plane.

For if those who lived during the Egyptian times or those who lived during slavery, those who lived and starved, they will still carry some of this frequency or some of this music within their soul. For you may look at each of our souls, each of our spirits as we have spoken of earlier, if you look at each spirit, you may look at it as a symphony, you may look at it as many different notes playing all at the same time, and if they are in harmony, then the spirit is harmonious. So you must pray for harmony within the spirit. You must pray for that which is the highest and best good, as this channel will say, but you must pray for harmony within yourself, within your spirit, and within that which is the earth plane in which you live on.

For many changes are coming throughout the planet, many changes are coming throughout the planet indeed, for as we slip into the next three or four months (this was recorded in December of 2014), the earth plane will be changing yet again, the frequencies will be changing. And as this channel has begun to

Book V   Ask Jesus

realize, there is much more falsehoods coming from this side, there are many more who are claiming to speak with us, there are many more that are claiming to talk with us, there are many more that are claiming to be channels bringing prophecy through about the things that are going to happen. And yes, yes they may be tuning in with their radio receiver signals (parable of the two-way radio), they may be tuning into a grid that says "I am Jesus, I am Christ, I am Peter, I am John, I am Zohar from the planet Zoloft..." and this is the different things that are coming into the earth plane at this time.

And as these channels are bringing this information in, not only are they speaking the words, the frequencies, into the earth plane, but every word that has ever been spoken, every act that has ever been done, is carried within the grid of the earth plane. For anything anyone does, while they are on earth, is stored and recorded within the grid. For when we allow the heavenly bodies to enter into the earth plane, we will allow for different heavenly bodies to infuse the earth with its knowledge, for we will allow the grid from Jupiter to infuse the planet Earth with its wisdom. We will allow the different bodies to infuse Earth with its wisdom.

At this moment there are many ascended masters that are working on infusing the grid with their knowledge, Saint Germane being one of them, Archangel Michael being another, Rafael being another (there are many that there are no names for, for there are "no names" that we can pronounce, but these are the three that the two of you would know by name). But there are many, many of us working on this side, working to make the earth stable. For it is very unstable at this time. It is going down the tubes, rather than up as we had planned.

*For there are many (everyday people) opening up, many seeing things that they had never seen before.... many feeling things and just as we had spoken of in the very first channelings in which the first book was written upon (*taping sessions commenced in early 2012 and were used for the basis of our first book, Answers: Heaven Speaks*), but was rewritten, there are many things about the grid but it was not put in those terms. And there are many aspects of those writings that are becoming true at this very time. For the earth is shifting and changing. In 8-10 months' time (*around August 2015*) the earth will go through an upheaval for one month. This will not be war and this will not be anything that your human mind would automatically go towards. This is more of a consciousness shift in that those who are still residing within the lower chakras and have not accelerated up past their emotional chakra, which would be below the belly button, they will feel sick. They will feel sick.*

Because all of these emotions that they have never felt, all these emotions that they have never expressed, all these emotions that they have never truly looked at, will make them feel sick. This is already beginning to happen. An example of this is the channel's mother. As you are seeing, many of the emotions that have never been dealt with are causing pain, causing frustration and causing physical damage. For when one is physically damaged, they look within to find help. They ask God for help. And the hopes are that from 8-10 months, if people are to begin to feel sick, but nothing is going to happen to them, they will begin to either reach out for God, reach out for help, reach out for healers, reach out for intuitives, reach out for people that can help them, counselors, psychologists, people who are here to help them understand and release these emotions.

*For in 10 months' time after this upheaval (*late Spring 2016*), the world will take another vibrational shift upward. There is a new string of children/souls coming into the earth plane at this* *time. There are 18,364 of these entering into the earth plane over the next six months (first half of 2015) that are very high vibrational souls created directly by ascended masters and godheads. These are souls that are brand new that were created directly by us, the ascended masters. So we are creating spirits and sending them into the earth plane to raise the vibration. We do not know whether this will cause a complete disruption to the grid, or if this will help things tremendously. So this is something, and we have always said, that they have treated earth as if it is an experiment, but really, everything is an experiment.*

83

(Peter and John)

Change in 'Spirit'... Change in Life

Marisa: Peter just cut in: "But really, everything is an experiment so just don't feel that, you know --."

Joe: Let me ask a question on that part. We know that angels can suddenly appear as human beings on the earth. So are these 18,364 new spirits, new souls, are they going to be born into babies, or are they going to show up as adult human beings?

(Jesus) This is a good question indeed. There are many babies/children that will and are being born. They will be born indeed. In fact, this is far over 70% of these children but a bit under 30% will be what many have called 'walk-ins' where a soul is suicidal, a soul wants to die, a soul does not want to be there anymore, so they barter and make a decision. They say, this body is still good, will somebody else take this? For understand and know that this is something that this channel has done, for she has traded spirits. For the spirit that resides within her now is of the same soul, of the same higher self, but a different spirit....

Joe: Oh, Marisa you were just talking about that...

(Jesus) ..... for the first spirit has left, but another spirit came in; same higher self, same soul but different spirit. The spirit that resided within this channel when she was born was a different one than resides within her now. For understand and know that this is where these abilities have come from, this is where the understanding has come from, because another aspect of her soul chose to step in and understand and see this, that ascended masters are souls so they may take a piece of themselves that are down here now that are tired (and replace that tired spirit and replace it with

something new). For the two of you are from godheads. The two of you are from our Father, our Father in heaven here.

Marisa: *And he's pointing at the Christ head right here.*

(Peter and John) You are children of this godhead, which is Christ, which is me. But understand that I am a direct offshoot of that, so you may look at it like this, the way that Christ broke off a piece of itself, made it into a spirit and I lived upon the earth. Ascended masters will do this. Christ will not do this (except for Jesus), but ascended masters will do this and they will come directly down. For there are many souls that are in treachery right now who are wanting to die, wanting to leave, not wanting to be here, but their human (talking clothes) still wants to be here. They are trapped inside a human that will not listen to them. So, many of these souls that we talk of, of the 18,000+ that will come in, speak with the higher self, and say; "This spirit does not want to be there anymore. Are you okay with us switching out?" And the spirit will say "Yay, get me out" and then comes a much more enlightened being. So you will hear of many, many people that were alcoholics, addicts, jailbirds, people from prison, people that have totally reformed their selves overnight or what seems like overnight and now they are channeling, they are channeling ascended masters; they are channeling enlightened beings; they are bringing this information through.

So the earth may say, "Those are drug addicts and losers and idiots, and those are murderers and killers. These are horrible people. How could they possibly be bringing through enlightened beings?" Well, it's because their souls have left the building and a new soul has entered. But understand and know that for many of these, it's a completely different soul.

So, there are many people, in fact 95% of human beings on the planet, do not have the same spirit their entire lifetime for they will change at some point or another. For there is many within a soul group of a higher self as you have been calling it, that will take turns living in the human because each want to have different experiences within it. For example, one aspect will live from zero to ten. The other aspect will live from ages 11-20. Sometimes there is more than one aspect within that human being at a time, experiencing this for there are not enough human beings for all the souls that want to experience life. For you must understand –

Marisa: And by the way, this is John and Peter talking, and Jesus is nodding at everything, because John just stepped in when he was talking about switching spirits. But Jesus is nodding yes to everything, but John got all excited and started talking. And now Jesus is coming back in and Jesus says ... he's like, "this is something that I did not want to share."

(Jesus) This is something that I did not want to share without explaining this completely, for this can be completely misunderstood. For people can say, "Oh no, I am not me anymore..." but this is not the way that it works. For understand and know that since we are all one, technically any aspect of anything that lives within anything is all one, but if you look upon this as a unified consciousness, each soul group is technically all one -- this is not even just the over-soul, the soul group -- we are all learning the same things; each within our soul group. I am part of your soul group for we are all learning the same things.

So any spirit that chose to enter into a human body at any time and began to reflect its wisdom through that spirit at that time would be okay. For in fact you may call upon aspects of your soul group to ask for information, and this is how this information is coming through. At times, because we are all part of this same soul group, we are entering in and we are bringing information *into the spirit in that which resides within Marisa [thank you for calling me Marisa] so that the information may be implanted into her brain, so that she may speak it, and teach it. For just understand and know that souls are interchangeable but they only, only can be interchanged if it is approved by the soul and the soul has it approved by the guide. This cannot happen without a spirit's approval. So in summary, in answer to your question, because angels can incarnate and appear, souls cannot appear this way, the way that you spoke of – physically manifesting themselves—but understand and know that some of the beings that are incarnating at this time are angels that are bringing in a higher frequency into the babies that are coming into the earth plane over the next 10 months (from December 2014 to September 2015).*

84

The Bible Speaks: Conversations with the New Testament Authors

(Peter and John)

Earth and God's Plan

(Rosemary)   So it's a fake world. It's like living in a movie and forgetting you're in a movie. It's really pretty funny, actually.

Marisa: *She's funny but serious too ....*

Joe: *That's what we wrote about. That's what we've been told because we're down here with amnesia. We don't know that we're spirit. We don't know that we came from Heaven first. We don't know that we've got all this protection around us. We've got half the world saying there is no god. And we have another half of the world that's saying....*

Marisa: *"Kill the other ones because they don't believe in our god."*

Joe: *.... yeah, exactly.*

Marisa: *So, she's saying that's all just ridiculous. She says they're.... she says God's plan says...and this is a quote from Jesus:*

(Jesus)   God's plan says that all men are created equal in that each soul has the same opportunity to grow within the earth plane. God's plan also states that as long as human beings are willing to -- as long as souls are willing to continue to incarnate on the earth plane, God's plan says that the earth will continue to exist. There are many that say that the earth will come to an end, the earth will float away, the earth will cease to exist. But this is

Book V   Ask Jesus

not the case. For, earth is a manifestation of the souls that created it and it is their choice.

Marisa: She (Rosemary) is basically saying earth isn't coming to an end, and that if earth comes to an end, all the souls will just make a new one, because we've just --- she's basically saying we just made it all up up here anyways, so if we destroy the earth, we'll just like --- like she's saying, like, it would be like if somebody was in a -- she's calling it a computer box. She's showing Joshua (Marisa's brother). Like, if Joshua was to destroy his videogame, he would just go do another one. And so she's saying it's kind of like, this is just a projection, and it's just the earth, and if it's destroyed we'll just go "okay, well here's another one." So she says she'll still be there, Jesus --- we'll all still be there. And, we'll be like, "Oh," and we'll go somewhere else and we'll forget that this earth even existed. She says the same thing happened with all the higher dimensional planets that we've lived on, that we've forgotten about.

The Bible Speaks: Conversations with the New Testament Authors

(Peter and John)

Jesus' Humble Message

Marisa: .... his hair is kind of short right now, and his beard is very cut. Doesn't seem like he ---oh he has a little bit -- his mustache and beard but it's very neatly trimmed. His eyes are going blue to green, to blue to green. So, let's see. Okay so Jesus says:

(Jesus)   My dear children, my dear brother and sister, I am so proud to say that you have accomplished so much in so little time. You have accomplished so much, and I have looked over, and I have watched over all of the proceedings in which you have done, and I must say that I bring forth pride and honor in that which you have established. For there are not many, there are not many that have the humility, that have the humility to take forth words that come forth from this side and bring them forth unto the earth without boasting, without bragging, without bringing forth the ego.

When I say this, I say this in terms of it is okay to be proud, it is okay to be proud, but it is not okay to say "guess what, we're the only ones that get to talk to Jesus. Guess what, we are so special that he has chosen us." This is something that many in the past have done. And this is something that ruins the message, ruins the message. For the message in which we are bringing through is that of a humble message, a humble message of peace, a humble message of love, and a humble message of joy. For understanding and knowing that each human being has love, peace and joy within them, is something that each human being needs to realize. For as we bring forth the authors, the authors in this book, and as we conclude the authors of this book, we say unto you that we are proud to have the earth plane understand and know that these authors were human, these authors were human. We laughed, we played, we joked. We were grumpy. We got angry. We bickered. All of these things happened, all of these things happened, and when people look upon those authors, when people look upon me as gods, as people who were not people, it makes it very hard to relate. Yes, it makes it very hard to relate.

So if people are able to relate to the characters, quote/unquote "characters" of this book that everybody, everybody knows about at least, or everybody knows the content of at least just a little bit, this makes it much more relatable, much more human, and people allow themselves to make mistakes. For what you must truly understand is that you must allow yourself to make mistakes. You must only look at the intention.

86

(Peter and John)

Never Assume How Someone Else Feels

(Jesus)   .... for Joe, you have felt guilty....

Joe: (I wrote an article in my newspaper column about an experience. A friend who I thought was agnostic or even atheistic related a beautiful story about a child who met Jesus and no one believed him since he was only six years old. But what this young child was told ended up coming true. So I wrote about it but also mentioned my friend by first name in the article. He took great deference to that and then disowned me as a friend. We had been playing golf together each Monday for almost ten years).

(Jesus)   You have felt sad about an action in which you have done to a friend, and I must say unto you, this is not something that you did that was bad. This is something that you must release. For you look at the intention. You look at the intention and you say, "I was glorifying God. I was showing that a friend was glorifying God." This is something that I was doing. This is the intention and I therefore release it. This is something that you should not be sad about. This is something that you should not feel bad about. Yes, you may feel bad that somebody is upset. You've apologized. This is okay.

But the earth plane must fully understand and realize that much of the bickering, much of the fights, much of the self-inflicted pain that people place upon them is guilt, that they did not do the right thing. But what people must understand is that there can be one person that does one thing to 10 people, and those 10 people will take it all differently. One will say, "Oh thank you so much for doing that. You are just amazing." Even if that person was a devout Catholic, they would look past that and say, "Wow, thank *you so much for mentioning me."* The next person would get angry. The next person would maybe be an atheist and they would say, *"Curse you, curse you but wow, my name sure looked great in the paper."* So you must understand that everybody will act differently, so you cannot hold yourself accountable to making every single person happy.

The only way that you understand life, Joe, and the only way that you understand life, Marisa, is through your own eyes, so you know how people will react based on how you would react. So I say this unto both of you. I say this unto both of you to please remember to understand and know that the way that you are seeing life is through your eyes. And, through your eyes never assume what somebody else feels. Never assume what somebody else will do, for they are not you. Keep communication lines open. Communicate with people. Communicate with people indeed, and understand and know that when you speak to people, when you speak to people tell them how you feel. Tell them how you feel. Understand and know that human beings are feeling creatures, feeling creatures, for we do not have the emotions that human beings have on this side. We do not have them until we enter into the earth plane and they are very, very hard to temper. They are very hard to control. And that is why the earth is where it is right now; because of the emotions, because of the emotions.

For if I can say one thing, one thing about the earth plane at this time, if I could say one thing that would pass upon words of peace, it is understand and know that your emotions dictate the life that you see. If you are angry, life does not look good. If you are happy, life looks good. So understand that the most important thing on the earth plane ever is not what you do, is not the amount of church you go to, it is not the amount of money you donate, it is not anything about what you do, it is how you feel. It is how you *feel and how you make the others around you feel. And if you feel that you are making them feel better but they do not feel better, this is not your fault. So understand that. Understand that. Forgiveness of self is the most important thing about living on the earth plane. For the only person, the only person that you must learn to forgive on a regular basis is yourself. For if you do not forgive yourself, you will think that others, you will think others are against you as well.*

87

(Peter and John)

Book V   Ask Jesus

The Council of 24

(John)   The 24 seated upon the thrones are those that I saw at the time as being the council of God, as being the left and right hand men of God. But....as I step forward now, [this is Jesus],

(Jesus)   As I step forward now I say unto you that there are souls, souls that have created, souls that have created the earth, souls that have created the universes, souls that are creators. For there are hierarchies in heaven, there are leaders so to speak in what you call heaven, and there are many, many that in these days in these spiritual times, will call the "white brotherhood." They are the ascended masters that come together; the white robed men that come together, to rule and watch over the throne of God or to watch over the hierarchy of that which is the energetic realms that surround earth and all of its inhabitants. For we have said many times before that there are 12 souls that created, 12 souls that created the earth. These souls came from greater souls which came from greater souls, which came from greater souls for God is never ending and God is ever-beginning. And, understanding and knowing that when there are councils that come together to bring justice unto earth, there are heads of families or soul heads that come together to bring this unto --.

Marisa: Hold on, Jesus keeps slipping out and then Christ in, and then John in. It's like they can't decide which one is going to stay in, or I can't hold the frequency. Hold on. What were you going to say?

Joe: Well, I was going to say that I've heard theologians say that the 24 are made up of the prophets from the Old Testament *including Moses, David, Jeremiah, Isaiah, Ezekiel, Joel, Daniel, etc. ...... and then all the apostles....*

(Jesus)   And this could be true in a sense, as you may look upon the over-souls, you may look upon these masters or these Thrones (a very high order of angels) as the creator souls. The creator souls that stand before.....(as we have said before, you come from a Throne's angel)....this is a master, a creator that has created beings and upon each family, upon each creator being is an assembly, or a council. For understand that for each soul family there is a council of 12. But for each soul, each soul, there is always a council of sorts. So understand that when John is being shown that there is a council of 24, this could very well be the over-soul of each one of these men. We will say that it is not exactly true, but to a certain extent, 12 of them are the prophets.

88

(Peter and John)

Book V   Ask Jesus

Masculine and Feminine

(Jesus)   I the Creator enter in and speak unto you through, as source, the creator. I show unto you that everything, everything in life, everything in life indeed, separates into two pieces – feminine and masculine, feminine and masculine; for when one is brought together and you see unto the earth plane as 12 souls creating a planet, 12 souls when they are separated and brought to their true form, they are separated into two – feminine and masculine. Therefore, the councils of these souls appear to be as two, even though there are truly only 12 souls that created this planet indeed; these 12 surrounding that which is the creator energy, the creator energy of Christ Lord himself and that which is the Holy Spirit combining together to create earth.

Joe: So when John is talking about 24 it's still the 12 creator spirits, but it's the female and masculine?

Marisa: Mm-hm.

Joe: So it's double?

Marisa: It is double. It is double for they are split at the top and there are two very different standpoints.

(Peter and John)

Revelation: John's Parable of the Golf Course

Joe: What the heck are the horses in Revelation?

(John) When we speak of the horses we speak of frequencies, we speak of, just as we have spoken of the barbed wire fence in the last conversations we've had, we speak of the barbed wire fence, we speak of different frequencies, we speak of different types of music so to speak that will activate different things. When we speak of the seals, we speak of the things that are broken within the human body, mind, and spirit that are able to begin to allow the spirit to ascend to higher aspects of its self. For Jesus was able to ascend through all seven of the energy bodies within man while in a human body, therefore becoming Christed.

When I speak of the lamb and the councils or the head of these souls bowing before the lamb, it is showing the gratitude that shows that a spirit or a personality has actually made it through, ascended, and become Christed within a world where no one had ever done this. For these 12 souls that created this planet were waiting upon someone to complete this, someone to break the seal; someone to say it is doable, it is passable.

John's Parable of the Golf Course

(John) Think of a game. Think of a game, Joe. You and 11 other souls create a golf course that seems very tough, there are very tough encounters to go through, but one golfer makes it, they pass, they pass, they make it through, and they get par on every single hole through storms, through desert weather, through shining sun, through sleet, through hail, and they make it through and this brings a celebration. This brings a celebration unto these

Book V   Ask Jesus

12 souls that have created this very difficult golf course for there are others who are trying to defeat (those trying to complete the golf course). There are others that are standing in front of the golfers. There are others that are playing very loud music behind the golfer when they are trying to concentrate and trying to make it through this golf course that you and the 11 other souls have created. For you are councils over this but you cannot really do much other than watch and wait as you have created this golf course, you have created these golfers to make it through this course quite perfectly. So when one makes it and makes it through, they are the lamb, they are Christed, and it breaks the seal, and says unto everybody else that is wandering this golf course that, "You can do this too!"

"And guess what, we are going to send help. We are going to send this music or these frequencies through this barbed wire fence that surrounds your golf course, and this will cause everybody to want to hit birdies (one under par). This will tell everybody to focus. This will tell everybody to turn their loud music off so that each person can concentrate while they are trying to hit the ball."

So understand and know that these horses are bringing help to the people of earth. The horses and the seals signify and represent the different chakras within the body of each human being that lives. For each human being has a root chakra and this root chakra brings foundation, it brings the home, it brings the security, it brings family, it brings all of the things that a child between the ages of zero and six need. For you see a child that is grasping for their parent's hand. They are developing their root chakra. There are many human beings that have never made it past this. All they worry about is their home. All they worry about is their car. All they worry about is their security. They do not have emotions, human emotions. For their spirit is kept within the root.

For when we bring peace unto this earth, this will bring peace unto these people so that they may begin to move up to the second seal, which is the emotional body. And understand that they will begin to understand and learn emotions. For a spirit to ascend into an ascended master as they call it, and eventually become Christed, they must experience life with all of their seven seals activated.

Joe: That's good because we've still got more seals and horses to go through. Alright, we've gotten through the white horse that wins many battles and gains the victory.

Book V   Ask Jesus

(Peter and John)

Halos

(Jesus)   -- the connection between God and spirit and human, bringing these two together-- For this is depicted in many old paintings where the saints appear to have halos. But it is because their energy body has broken the seal of the seventh, the seventh chakra upon the top of the head, appearing to have a crown upon their head, appearing to have a halo around their head.

The Bible Speaks: Conversations with the New Testament Authors

(Peter and John)

Witchcraft

Joe: And it was the word "witchcraft" that caused me to write down my question. I'm asking Jesus again, by us communicating with him would that be considered witchcraft?

(Jesus) Witchcraft is manipulating the energy, changing the energy within someone, preferably their root chakra. So you may place evil thoughts just as you say prayers for someone's highest and best good, you may place evil thoughts within their energy centers, within their body, that will say, "You will lose all your money, you will love me, you will hate him..." This is witchcraft. This is energy work that is done without permission to another based on the mind of the one doing this. What you are doing is not witchcraft.

Book V   Ask Jesus

(Matthew and Mark)

Communication via the Holy Spirit

Marisa: *He says that he lives on every floor, a piece of him does, and that there's a piece of him that can communicate with anybody on the earth plane, because that's why he made himself available through the Holy Spirit. The Holy Spirit is like a little internal GPS honing device. It's like a little walkie-talkie that can communicate with him. And even if they're down in the depths of hell, whether they're on the earth plane or in the ethers of the astral plane, they can still call out for his help and be forgiven. The problem with the ones on the lower planes is they think they'll be judged so they don't call Jesus for help.*

(Jesus)   And this is true. This is true my child, this is true my brother, my sister. But what one must understand and be able to differentiate is that with the Holy Spirit, with this beacon of light that each carries within them, they can communicate with God, they can communicate with their soul, they can communicate with anything that has a Holy Spirit, which is everything. So this is not just a way to communicate with me, which this may have come through as the Holy Spirit is a way to communicate with only me. The Holy Spirit is what this channel is using to communicate with that which is this side, as you call it, the "other side" (and everything in it). The Holy Spirit is the walkie-talkie within each human being that can communicate with the upper realms.

Marisa: *So he's saying that he can lower his vibration so that he can channel – I can channel him.*

Book V   Ask Jesus

(Matthew and Mark)

On a Mission

Joe: Did he know he was God before – before his baptism, or did he just act on what he had been told by his – from his mother, from his birth?

(Matthew) He did not know he was God and never claimed to be God.

Joe: That's different than in the Bible, because in the Book of John, we know that he tells people that he is –

(Matthew) He is speaking of the spirit inside. He is not speaking of Yeshua the man. He is speaking of the incarnated spirit inside of him as he speaks with that higher aspect of himself through channeling.

Joe: (Interrupting Matthew and telling Marisa) Now remember, we need Jesus to jump in at any time here to correct anything being said.

Marisa: Yeah, he will.

(Jesus) I have an innate knowing...

Marisa: This is Jesus

(Jesus) *There was an innate knowing from the time that I was born. There was an understanding that I was here to do something just as both of you understood that you are here to do something. You have always had that urge. You have always had that curiosity. You have always looked at the stars and said, "Is this really all that there is?" So you have had a knowing. You have had a knowing that these days were coming, that this time is coming, that this ministry was coming. So you did know.*

You do know and this is the same way that I knew that there was something, something there. This was my reason for taking my travels to India and to Egypt and to different places of the world to understand and learn the healing arts and to understand how human beings in the ancient times were able to heal themselves and to pray for themselves and to not have to go to an intermediary between human beings and God. I learned just like every other human being learns how to associate oneself with God. I studied and I learned. This is not something where I was born and I automatically knew everything, but I did know. I did know I was on a mission.

94

(Matthew and Mark)

Parable of the Diamond

Marisa: Okay, so let's see – oh, I didn't finish the prayer. Let's see here. Okay. Someone named Rosemary is here from the Bible. I don't know this Rosemary. She said she lived back then. She had a tough childhood.

(Rosemary) Jesus told me the demons weren't placed on there by God, that they are placed on there by man; that there were demons around men and the only way to stay away from the demons was to trust in the Father and trust in the Father's love to surround, to surround us all. He gave us a simple parable. He compared us, he compared us to, as we have said, the salt of the earth, but he also compared us to a piece of coal and a stone. He said, "Look at the stone. Look at the crystal, the crystal and the stone –

Marisa: Hold on. She's showing me something. No it's not a crystal it's a....

Parable of the Diamond

(Rosemary) .... a diamond." He compared us to a diamond and he said the coal is around the diamond and the spirit is inside, and when this coal can fall off then the diamond can show, but if

we take the pressure and the love of the unconditional love that is carried within that of the Christ, we will then become Christed one day and this love will just "poof" remove the coal.

Joe: To reveal the diamond....

(Rosemary) To reveal the diamond so that we feel like the diamond and we shine like the diamond and we are the diamond, and this is what I carried with me as I felt like the diamond. I released the coal and I released the demons, and this is something that I was forever grateful for and I will be forever grateful for and I will continue to teach his words and I will stay on the earth plane in this time, in this space to help the evolution of the planet, because people do not understand or put behind the teachings the excitement and the joy and the effervescent love that is expanding throughout the world.

Book V   Ask Jesus

95

(Matthew and Mark)

Rosemary on Jesus

(Rosemary) They put Jesus up as God and he spoke his words of wisdom and he shared these words. He was funny. People laughed. People could not stop laughing around his presence (a little exaggeration as Jesus mentions later). He made jokes. He said these, as you say, parables, but he was constantly lighthearted. We sang and we danced.

There are many religions that say that you cannot sing and dance. This is absolutely ludicrous. This is ridiculous, because we carry the childlike presence of fun and joy and excitement. And this is why I'm so excited to share this for as he (Matthew) spoke earlier, he spoke so seriously, because he came in later on and he heard the words and he heard the joy and he heard the excitement but had been so unhappy his entire life, so he translated (his accounts to you) through a very serious way. Although many things were lifted from him, this was a way that he brought these words in. And there is much joy and much excitement and much pleasure that was taken out of the words of the Bible and turned into such a serious book, turned into such a serious book that when one reads it they do not get joyful. They get joyful at hoping that *they are good enough because they are reading it, that God will love them because God will judge them if they don't.*

There are so many more books that many of the ladies that I knew of wrote and they were not put in the Bible. They were not put in the Bible at all. I have watched over the years from here on this side as a teacher of Christ, of Christianity. I have watched how these things have been skewed and changed. I can tell you things that you probably wouldn't even believe because I have kept in tune with this religion.

Book V   Ask Jesus

96

(Matthew and Mark)

Life and the Times Aren't So Different

Marisa: Hang on, here's Jesus .....

Joe: Okay. Thanks, Jesus. Thank you, very much for letting us ....

(Jesus)   The "thank you" must go to the souls in which you carry. The "thank you" must go to the drive in which you have for I just bring to you the story, the story of life, the story of creation and the story of love for as this channels through this channel, as this channels through into the words, into the pen, into the fingers in which type you will see, you will see that life will be brought to these words. Not everything that comes through will be things that are used, but everything that comes through are things that will teach you to understand that life was just the same as it is now back then.

It was not something that was very dry just as the historians have made it sound. As Rosemary has said, it was eventful and fun and exciting and there was tragedy, but tragedy was followed by victory and these things are brought through.

There is so much depression that is circled around the story of my life, the story of my life, and what I want to do is help people to understand it was a joyous time and yet the people say, "The martyr, the martyr, he died for us, he died for us. Oh, we're so sad, we're so sad. We're so bad. He had to die for us because we're so evil."

This is not the way that things should be portrayed in any way. They should be portrayed as; "He (Jesus), he worked so hard to learn how to heal people, and he raised his vibration, and you can do this too." And by being killed, this was a symbolism of what the human man, the human savage beast will do to those who are different than them, will do to those who rise above them in vibration, because they are fearful of the things that they do not understand, just as the church is fearful of the things in which you two do. So if it was these times, if it was the Bible times, they would probably kill you two also – because they do not want to hear what you have to say.

Joe: *Yipes! .... well, there are some people today that would like us to shut up and go away .... at least they don't want to kill us .... as far as I know!!*

(Jesus)   *This is exactly – you may not have been hung upside down on a cross, but this is something that you would probably be killed for, because anything out of the rhythm of what the church brings in, this is something that falls out of that pathway, out of the control and out of the jurisdiction of them. So please understand, my sister, please understand my brother, that we are partners in this. We are a team, and as soon as we can look at ourselves as a team and less as "Oh, mighty Lord, God, please give us this information and forgive us of all our sins," yes, this is true. This is what the Father does, but I am, I am a mouthpiece to this earth. I am an incarnation of this piece on earth to help people understand that we are all equal.*

We are all equal indeed, and we can all practice the miracles of life and healing. And one day, one day under my rule and under the rule of the Masters in which I work with and the Masters in which you work with, this world will be fully self-sufficient. Human beings will heal upon touch with each other. Nobody will be sick and old. It would be like the other planets in which we have touched upon in past sessions, for I have been here for each session prior to this, but this channel is unable to see me. Please understand that I have been giving a lot of the information in which you received in your (first) book (Answers: Heaven Speaks). You need to understand this, for each time you've called in the Christ Light, you called me in. So see this and know this, that the information that has come through is very valid and it is time, it is time to see the recognition and yourselves that you are able to connect with these higher dimensions and this is good. We are proud, we are proud of both of you, and we are proud of the guides in which help you. We thank them and we thank you. We will protect you throughout this week until we meet again. We are very proud of you. Please remain grateful, happy, humble, yet proud because you are doing good things, and for this we are proud.

Marisa :   That was your higher self that switched over at the end of Jesus's statement. It was like Jesus and then at the very end it was like your higher self jumped in. He's huge.

97

(Matthew and Mark)

'I am Proud of the Human Race'

(Jesus) Dear brother and sister, the aspect that you are channeling, the aspect that you are tapping into of each of these fellow men are aspects of that which is their physical existence. This was bringing the energy to explain how an understanding, the imagery or the way that the relationship showed itself on the Earth-plane (over two thousand years ago). Please note that when we call in these energies and we bring in these energies to this channel, there is only one to be brought in at a time or otherwise there is a chance that deception will come through.

Joseph: Good. I'm happy he's warning us about that.

(Jesus) So when there is more than one (Apostle in here) there is conflict. For one may have another opinion about the other in this channel because tapping into the upper dimensional soul planes, this is something that far surpasses what most human beings can do. So, when tapping into these higher dimensions you are tapping into the soul so to speak; the aspects of the self that is evolved, but remember that the soul is the totality of every physical incarnation. So yes, only one at a time in one place so that this channel can handle them without interruption.

I come in with the ability to lower my vibration not only to this channel but to every human being on the planet as well for I am able to lower myself down to the human (energy level). This is how I reappeared to people (after the crucifixion) for I was in the spirit world, brought my density back and appeared to them and this is how I operated. For, I learned how to continue my learning as well as my teaching since then. I have grown very proud of the human race but, there is a need for a Band-Aid so to speak, something to hold it together because there are those who are 'bleeding' to death and they do not feel as if there are any Band-Aids to patch them up. For understanding that each one of us are a piece of Christ, each one of us are created by Christ and only through evolution of the soul, only through progressing through the levels so to speak will help that soul, that higher self, that spirit, to become Christed and then once again, to return back to home. This is what I have accomplished throughout eternity after I was Christed.

98

(Matthew and Mark)

The Bible is a Book of Faith

Joe: Jesus, you said you will shut all this down if I go negative or if I tried to change.... He's (Mark) detracted from the Bible and could persuade people not to trust the Bible.

(Jesus) Many things are changed but with the guidance of God over those who rewrote the book or condensed the book. One may believe that those who wrote the book or rewrote the book were putting in that which was only positive so that people would agree with and worship me as Christ for there were many things written in many of the books that carried a negative connotation toward that which is the one true God. This is not to say that Mark said anything negative but in the churches eyes this was. So what better than to take all of the positive aspects of his writing and put them into a condensed version of what he wrote?

So you do not need to speak of the fact that the Bible is wrong. You may say that man put this information into books to make it more understandable for the people at the time. But there must be an understanding that there are holes and there are more. There was more written. This is not saying that the Bible is wrong.

Book V   Ask Jesus

This is saying that information is missing and this is okay to express. For everybody, even the most devout Christians as you call them, have doubts about why there are holes in the stories in the Bible. The Bible is really just a book of faith, a book of understanding, and that which God is, and I was the messenger. The book was inspired by God and brought to the people to bring faith.

99

(Matthew and Mark)

Mark's take on Jesus

Joe: *Rosemary mentioned after the Matthew interview that Jesus wasn't portrayed accurately because he (actually) had a good sense of humor and he liked laughter and he kept people happy and laughing. Is that something that Mark saw? He was not in the inner circle of Jesus and the Apostles but rather he stood afar or was a part of a larger group that followed Jesus around. Was Jesus a light-hearted happy person?*

(Mark) *Absolutely! He was joyous and happy. He was serious when he needed to be but that was just in congruence with someone who felt they were unworthy. He would explain to them that the forgiveness of self is the key to existence for when one forgives oneself they are able to be free.*

100

(Matthew and Mark)

God Would Die for Us

(Jesus)   *(As referenced in "Heaven Speaks") ... every soul prior to incarnation creates a life plan that is approved by Christ and is referenced to as the chart or the life chart, the plan.*

(Mark)   I lived out my days and I prepared the message in which was to be told to the world. I accomplished this and I accomplished it well and now I stand on this side indeed and watch as the world can at times not understand the words in which we are told, not understand the words in which were written, but this is okay because for the most part the message was brought across in love and light, in God, in source, and the Holy Spirit, and that which is bringing this sixth sense into the human beings to bring messages through. This is one thing that many people did not understand of me, in that many of the messages that were transpiring through the thoughts that I had were not of this world.

For, I do not live in this world, nor did I live in this world prior to incarnating in this world. For, I live in other dimensions, other planets, other planetary systems, other universes, but was part of this world prior to it being the world that it is today. For many call it the lost city of Atlantis. Many call it many other things. But as a medium aged soul, I lived in the more developed world which resided on earth and learned many trades, learned how to heal, learned how to educate, and I learned the science of the earth. So when I returned for this incarnation as Mark, I came with an inner knowing and I came with the guides in which I worked with prior. I came with the high priest. I came with the scientists. I came with a minister. I came with a scholar. I came with all of these guides in which I worked with when I was on the earth plane before. So these are the wise men that I speak of. These are the wise men I speak of indeed, and these are the ones that I channeled, that I wrote with, that I dedicated my life to, and they were the ones that helped me to see what needed to be said and what needed to be done for I truly did have a strong connection with many of the people that I met and became friends with.

So my message to the world was what came through in the text that you read today. It was not necessarily important where I grew up or what I did or where I went. Rather it was the message of love and light that came through, to help people to understand that a man can dedicate himself to the world and die for the sins of others and not in the sense that one man dies and everybody gets off on what they do, but to show, to show people, to show people that dying, dying does take away the sins that you lived in this lifetime, but dying, dying on a cross for some sins helps people to see that when they think life is really that bad and they are feeling greed and lust and anger and power struggle, and they are feeling all of these things that the human mind feels over things that really aren't that big of a deal, they see death as something that reminds them that... "Maybe my problems aren't that big of a deal anymore; maybe I should forgive my neighbor, maybe I should forgive my friend for at least I'm not dying." And this was kind of a reminder to the people. This was a reminder.

Book V   Ask Jesus

And when this, this crucifixion happened, when Jesus quote/unquote "died for everyone's sins," it was to show that God loves us no matter what. God would die for us. And although I do not say Jesus is God, and although Jesus does not say Jesus is God, God shows that God would die for his children just as a parent would die for their children. And people must see God being merciful, not God being evil. And many people saw God as an evil god at that time. What God wanted was for people to see God as compassionate and not to be feared. For, many stories were told, many stories were told indeed, in that which is the Bible, the New Testament and the Old, whereby making God sound ruthless, evil, mean, vengeful, wrathful. And these are not any of the traits of God. These are the traits of man.

The Bible Speaks: Conversations with the New Testament Authors

101

(Matthew and Mark)

Charisma

Joe: Charisma. *I think I've described it to people, as I've explained to people what I'm learning and hearing from Jesus and those who followed him is that his charisma is off the charts. Jesus will never call it that himself. That is what I'm going to try to get out of all of these interviews and what their take is.*

(Jesus)   I came into a body and I came into a mind that would understand that free will was a key, but understand that personality is one of the most important things while in any egoic run body for if one has the best personality in the world they may tell lies and others will believe them. If somebody has no personality at all they may tell truths and nobody will listen to them. So knowing that, the people in whom I would be born into I knew that there must be a charismatic nature to that human being which I lived in.

So yes I will admit to the charisma as a positive attribute to the ministry for if there was no charisma there is no charm as you would say in these days. There would not have been such an

impact for people who are attracted to the light, and what I brought forth was for them to understand not to worship me but to worship the God inside each and every one of us. And this was the teachings in which I brought. But human beings, just as they have done for millions and millions of years, tend to worship their fellow brothers and sisters if they are further along their path than others. This would be like first graders in elementary school worshipping a sixth grader because they passed school. When really they are just a fellow student and they are not any worse than the sixth grader, they are just younger.

So know that when I brought this information through to the writers of the Bible, when I brought the information through to the ceremonious events that would occur, people needed to see what being influenced by spirit or of the spirit would do for a human existence, for if people were trained today, they could do exactly the same things that I was able to do and more, for the Earth carried a lower vibration at that time, and it was much harder back then to access the higher vibration spirit, the holy spirit, the soul's consciousness, and all the way up. So know that it was very important that I was not to be worshipped because that takes the glory from God.

102

(Matthew and Mark)

'I Came to Change the World'

Joe: In one passage that is in a number of the (Bible) books, primarily John......I will get into that when we get into our interview with John...they have asked...your disciples asked you; had you seen the father? Had you met the father? Of course I'm paraphrasing here. And your response was...as you see me you see the father. And again I am paraphrasing. So you taught them that you were not God but that by accepting you they were seeing the father.

(Jesus)   Each one of us is God and as the consciousness raises there are more of the attributes that come whereby if one, if one is spiritually young just as we have said in first grade they will not see the positive influence they can have using the power of God within each of us. You must understand that the church had to make a martyr out of someone so the people would feel guilty enough to worship and repent.

Book V   Ask Jesus

This is something that is completely off the subject but at the same time very much on the subject in that yes, the Holy Spirit resides within each person. Yes, each person is a human soul living in a physical body. Yes, I taught how to in the terms of what the channel may use, raise the vibration of the human existence whereby to pray, channel, and directly communicate with the Godhead within each of us and this was taught to the followers, the 32, and they were able to communicate with that which was their higher self or that which was the Holy Spirit. And this is what I taught. This is what I taught to teach each person; that they can do just as I did and more. And yet when the church came to write these things, many things, when the church came many things were changed. So understand that the understanding of God within each of us was that which when you open your heart to God, when you release your sins, when you allow yourself to feel the Holy Spirit you will become more God-like, more Christ-like and this is why I came down to teach this for I have lived through millions of years of a very old soul evolved through third dimensional worlds into Christhood and could not just sit on the other side watching as human beings killed each other; for I came into this life with an understanding that I was going to change the world, and this has happened. My guides helped me through, my soul family members, and to the humans at that time, even to the humans at this time, the abilities I had, which anyone can have with the persistence of working with spirit and releasing just as I have said, releasing the negativity about oneself and sins so to speak can become just like the way that I as spirit was residing in a physical body. Does this make sense?

Joe: It makes sense. The one thing I question is, Jesus you say that everyone can do what you can do and you taught them.

103

(Matthew and Mark)

Human Nature vs. Enlightenment

(Jesus) What they are taught is to understand and bring in that worthiness for when one believes I have talents that have not surfaced they will have more faith within themselves, and more of an understanding that they will want to move forward in utilizing these gifts. They may not be a master even before they die, but the recognition of knowing that the Holy Spirit and the abilities of Christ are within each person helps to allow them to love themselves.

Joe: If you only need to have the faith that the Holy Spirit is there for them all the way, all the time and that they need to learn to love themselves....

(Jesus) Yes, not by pointing a finger saying, at least I'm not them, or at least I'm not like that. This is not the road to enlightenment.

Book V Ask Jesus

Joe: *Yeah I just thought of what you taught; "before you take the speck out of your neighbor's eye first take the plank out of yours." In other words, someone shouldn't be criticizing that person because what he's doing is even worse!*

(Jesus) But it's human nature and that is what humans do, and this is the whole divine creation and the experiment on this planet where divine human souls just as yourself can incarnate into a world that is run by selfish greed and understanding between light and dark where many will take dark because it is more fun, but being a soul that incarnates into these animalistic creatures is something that is quite a challenge and a blessing. I owe all of this to those who believed. If none had believed, then nothing would have happened after I left. I left for many years (while living as a human) and trained my emotional, mental and spiritual bodies so that when I returned to the town in which I was born I would be able to teach other people.

104

(Matthew and Mark)

We Love the Human Beings

Joe: I keep hearing your words. I know you don't want me to detract from the Bible and we don't want to go negative. You said otherwise you are going to "shut it (these conversations) down". So I don't want to shut it down. I don't want you to shut this down. I just want to put out the book you want us to put out. I'm going to do the best I can. Marisa, God bless her that she can talk to all of you guys, is just so amazing.

(Jesus) This is a blessing for us as well to keep the memory alive and to keep the faith strong on the planet for we have chosen as Masters and as Christed beings to remain in the realms of the human beings. Many have traveled to other planets. Other universes began to create their own worlds but there are many of us who stayed behind to help the human beings on earth to evolve for we cherish the human beings. We love the human beings.

Book V   Ask Jesus

Joe: We love you too Christ. Jesus we love you.

(Jesus)   And I was a man walking and living the temptations and the rule of the egoic mind, the intellectual mind over the spirit so I can relate to those on the Earth-plane at this time. For again I am not just an idol to be worshipped, I am someone who may be called on at any time just as we have spoken about already. See me as a minister speaking through a microphone, and as each person tunes in to this ministry whether they are listening or not, their subconscious mind will hear it, and this will raise their vibration, and the negativity will fall off. They will forget that there is negativity even on them and they will become believers. So this is a constant battle so to speak getting the human beings to understand. The same story has to be used over and over and over again in history and that is because human beings want to believe.

The conversations in which we have with each person on this planet are a conversation in which they receive. They just may not consciously receive this. Many receive it in dreams. Many receive it through messages throughout the day. As one has explained in the past you may have looked at every message in which we send to each field as a message left in their field written on a little piece of paper. As this little piece of paper flies around and runs into the head, the head will then say, I know what I need to do, and this is because we've been delivering these messages.

Joe: I feel that.

105

(Matthew and Mark)

The Way, The Truth and The Light

Joe: Everybody wants to know when Jesus is coming again but I don't want to ask the questions now. I don't want an answer.

Marisa: He is already here.

Joe: I know but everybody is waiting for another David. They want to see a big strong Jesus with holes in his hands and holes in his feet and a hole in his side from a spear.

Marisa: Why?

Joe: I don't know. It's in John's book of Revelation.

Marisa: As proof?

Joe: Yes. They want Jesus to come and wipe out everybody that doesn't believe in Christ.

Marisa: *That will never happen.*

Joe: *Christians believe that... In John 14:6 it says Jesus that you are the way, the truth and the light... It is said that Jesus said: "I am the way, the truth, and the light and no one gets to the father but through me." So Christians believe that anybody who does not believe in you will go to hell and I think they are waiting for the day you are going to come to the Earth and you are going to wipe out all those people who don't believe in you and leave a paradise for the remaining Christians. I just kind of wag my head...*

(Jesus)   It is absolutely not true in that it brings in an understanding that we are judgmental on this side. We may have judged in the human bodies in which we lived, but who says that one believes or does not really believe? There are many more than 70% of the Christians today that don't really believe. Their ego believes but their intellectual mind does not. Their spirit wants to believe but it doesn't understand it. So 70% of these church goers that do not believe are in worse off shape than those that don't believe, that don't go to church because there is a contradiction going on, a frustration when one does not believe because they do not understand. So as we bring in the information that we bring through to you and to many other channels, the things that are expressed are things that add knowledge to teachings and the understandings of that which was the past.

There are so many that already shamed the Bible. There are so many that say this (the Bible) is not God's word. They say this is man's word which we do not totally disagree with. But it is the understanding that we are here to acknowledge what was written as a historical paper, a historical writing and an understanding of who God is so when I say that you must go through me to get to the father, I spoke of the Christ.

106

(Matthew and Mark)

Parable of the Tennis Ball

Marisa: *Here's Rosemary channeling Jesus.*

(Rosemary)   *Just look at the spirit, or the soul or the higher self as the higher piece of you and understand that within that piece of you imagine a tennis ball cut in half and that tennis ball inside of it has a smaller tennis ball that fits perfectly in it. So there is a little rim inside and then another smaller tennis ball and another smaller tennis ball and then a small and small and smaller all the way down. If you look at that as your higher self, your spirit, your soul for each layer, if you look at that as the Christ within you, this covers everything and this is what Jesus taught.*

Joe: *Oh, that is nice and easy.*

(Rosemary)   *If you look at this, look at every single aspect. For when you ask, I heard earlier when you asked, when am I able to*

Book V   Ask Jesus

talk to my soul? You can talk to your soul right now. You can talk to your soul. You can talk to your soul group, you can talk to your over-soul, you can talk to Christ and you can talk to God whether you can hear them back, that is a different story. We are much easier to hear as we have incarnated as guides and we are easier to hear at times than words directly from God. But God sends these messages with angels. With angels many a time, so you will get the messages regardless. But please look at that piece of God inside of you. It is a multi-layered ball and when you utilize that you do not need to differentiate between, I'm calling my spirit, I'm calling my higher self, I'm calling my soul, oh wait no, no, I need to call in Christ or wake the over-soul!

Marisa: She's being exuberant. She is making fun of it (how we pray).

Joseph: Ha, ha, ha. That is okay. I don't mind.

(Rosemary)   Well what we need to do is to understand that all of these levels are God and you are God just as I am God, but I understand that Eden just said, "You know what Rosemary, they need to understand it that way otherwise they are not going to understand. (Eden is one of Joseph's guides)

Marisa: Eden is getting all... not defensive, but just kind of like...

(Rosemary)   It may have been easy for you to understand when you are there because the consciousness was lower to just go okay God, but Eden is saying that there are a lot of people on the Earth-plane right now that need to understand the hierarchy because they will understand how they were created and where they came from.

Joseph: Well we did the foundation in our first book I think.

Marisa: Yeah.

Joseph: I mean it is not a perfect book, but the foundation is there.

Marisa: Yeah, the book is good.

Joseph: I know; I don't want any negativity in this at all.

(Eden) There won't be any negativity but we must share with you the exact information so that you may understand how to place the information so that it is correct, but not negative for we do not want to draw any Christians, true Christians away from Christianity. But there will be a world with no religion in the near future. Within the next few hundred years, religion will not exist. Religion is laws. Religion is government. Religion is power, control and undermining the human being of what they are capable of. And assigning people who are Godlier than another because they say they are and having people go to that person in order to connect with God when God is as Rosemary said a tennis ball surrounded by another tennis ball and another tennis ball inside, in layers like an onion and when that piece of God inside is resonated with and spoken to it speaks back. For do not look at God as outside of you, look at God as something somewhere everywhere and the inside of that tennis ball has a walkie-talkie, and this walkie-talkie communicates directly with God wherever God may be. So technically, listening to the inside of you is where you are getting the information, not from the outside, so this must be understood as well and as soon as people can understand that God does not judge, you do not need to go to another human being in order to connect with God, the world will be a completely different place, and this is what we look forward to.

107

(Matthew and Mark)

Jesus' Closing

Marisa: *Jesus has something else to say .....*

(Jesus)   *Understand that I love both of you. I love both of you. I am very proud to say that we have worked on this project together, we have worked on this together, and the world will see this. The world will see this, for we are working on a project on the television box, we are working on this project at this moment, trying to bring to the earth plane that which is the words of me, the words of spirit, as they say, and bring the light, the light which is imbued within each and every single one of us to the surface so that people, people that would never be affected by these words will be affected by them. For this is something that both of you are a part of, both of you are a part of, and we appreciate the fact that you*

have as foot soldiers volunteered to enter into a chaotic place to bring such peace to the world.

Please know that we are so proud, we are so proud of you. We applaud you. We applaud you indeed, and we say unto you, we love you, we bless you, and we will talk to you soon.

Authors Page

Joseph Patrick Moris Marisa Patrice Moris and Poochie

Joseph P. Moris is an author and columnist. Joe co-authored with his daughter Marisa their first book entitled: *"Answers: Heaven Speaks."* Joe also writes a lifestyle column for the North Coastal San Diego County newspaper *"The Coast News"* and is currently a semi-retired real estate broker/owner for *Coastal Country Real Estate* in Encinitas, CA and living part-time in Puerto Vallarta and also Playa Los Cocos near San Blas in mainland Mexico. Joe also studied and earned Bachelor Degrees in 1977 in Political Science and Economics at the University of California, Santa Barbara. He is also a US Army veteran of the Vietnam War era.

Book V   Ask Jesus

Marisa P. Moris is the founder and director of *Discover Intuition*. Marisa co-authored, with her father Joe, "Answers: Heaven Speaks." She is a teacher, a spiritual intuitive and "clairvoyant channel" who helps her clients find their true inner spiritual self and yet....so much more!

Marisa has also co-authored the Skeptic series of books dealing with subjects such as the Universe, Intuition, Tao and much more with author/publisher/film maker William Gladstone.

www.ingramcontent.com/pod-product-compliance
Lightning Source LLC
Chambersburg PA
CBHW070140100426
42743CB00013B/2773